P9-BYV-956

What Readers Are Saying about
MAKING YOUR CHILDREN'S MINISTRY THE BEST HOUR OF EVERY KID'S WEEK

Today, the single remaining common interest or entrance point for non-churched people in the life of a church is their child. And I believe there's going to be a whole new run, a whole new day, a whole new revolution in children's ministry. This book is all about that revolution!

Bill Hybels

This book is a must-read for every children's ministry leader. Sue Miller offers invaluable principles that I believe are transferable to every church that seeks to effectively invest in the next generation with life-changing impact.

Linda Unruh, Director of Children's Ministry,
The Meeting Place, Winnipeg, Manitoba, Canada

Anyone who is serious about impacting the heart of a child will want to read *Making Your Children's Ministry the Best Hour of Every Kid's Week*. Sue Miller and David Staal not only challenge children's ministries to become more relevant, they also provide a strategy for meeting this challenge that has proven effective in churches of all sizes. The principles presented reflect the heart of seasoned leaders committed to sharing critical insights and contagious passion. We now have a new standard for any ministry that believes kids really matter to God.

Reggie Joiner, Executive Director of Family Ministry
at North Point Community Church, Atlanta, Georgia

The dream is possible ... and promising! Miller and Staal have filled their book with compelling stories, tested techniques, humble admissions of failure, glorious examples of success, and encouragement to dream big. If you've dreamed of a children's ministry where children beg to come to church, applying principles from this book will make your dream come true! This is a must-read for every children's minister around the world!

Christine Yount, Executive Editor, *Children's Ministry Magazine* and author of *With All Their Heart*

MAKING YOUR
CHILDREN'S
MINISTRY
THE
BEST HOUR
OF EVERY
KID'S WEEK

Sue Miller *with* David Staal

Forewords by
Bill Hybels & George Barna

ZONDERVAN™

GRAND RAPIDS, MICHIGAN 49530 USA

WILLOW
Willow Creek Resources

ZONDERVAN™

Making Your Children's Ministry the Best Hour of Every Kid's Week
Copyright © 2004 by Willow Creek Association

Requests for information should be addressed to:
Zondervan, *Grand Rapids, Michigan 49530*

Library of Congress Cataloging-in-Publication Data

Miller, Sue
    Making your children's ministry the best hour of every kid's week / Sue Miller with David Staal; forewords by Bill Hybels & George Barna.
      p. cm.
    ISBN 0-310-25485-X
    ISBN-13: 978-0-310-25485-0
    1. Church work with children. 2. Staal, David. I. Title.
BV639.C4 M55 2004
259'.23 –dc22

                                    2004002277

This edition printed on acid-free paper.

All Scripture quotations, unless otherwise indicated, are taken from the *Holy Bible: New International Version®*. NIV®. Copyright © 1973, 1978, 1984 by International Bible Society. Used by permission of Zondervan. All rights reserved.

All rights reserved. No part of this publication may be reproduced, stored in a retrieval system, or transmitted in any form or by any means—electronic, mechanical, photocopy, recording, or any other—except for brief quotations in printed reviews, without the prior permission of the publisher.

Interior design by Tracey Moran

Illustrations by Liz Conrad

Printed in the United States of America

---

08 09 10 /❖ DCI/ 12 11 10

To the unstoppable Willow Creek volunteers
who make Promiseland the best hour
of every kid's week—you guys rock!

I thank my God every time I remember you.
Philippians 1:3

CONTENTS

FOREWORD
BY BILL HYBELS

I met Sue Miller when we were both carefree teenagers. We double-dated one night in high school because Sue was dating a good friend of mine who needed my wheels, and I needed to move my fuel gauge a little to the right of E. A five-dollar bill solved both of our problems.

If you would have told me that night that I would be writing a book foreword for my friend's date three decades later, everyone in the car would have belly laughed! None of us had a clue what amazing twists God had in store for our lives' paths. Sue and I both wound up marrying the people we were dating at that time. The four of us stood up in each other's weddings. And, the four of us teamed up to start a student ministry that eventually birthed Willow Creek Community Church . . . only God!

Of all Willow's ministries, one that has given me immense joy over the years is our children's ministry called Promiseland. Involving almost three thousand children per week, and requiring the participation of over one thousand volunteers, Promiseland continues to be our church's single most important ministry to reach families.

Sue Miller has provided point leadership for Promiseland for the last thirteen years. Under her leadership, hundreds of children have placed their trust in Jesus Christ, and thousands more have driven their roots deeper into the faith. Through Promiseland, countless parents have learned how to pray with their children and talk with them about spiritual matters. Adults all over our church have learned how to serve the very ones Jesus scooped up into his lap and blessed.

It wasn't long until churches around the world began calling us to learn about Promiseland. Sue was initially very reluctant to give any counsel to other children's ministry leaders because she always felt that our own ministry still had too many challenges to overcome. While I respected her concerns, I finally convinced her to hold a conference for those who were curious about doing kid's church a new way. She agreed on one condition: right up front she would tell all those attending that Promiseland was a work in progress and still had a long way to go. Her admission only endeared her more to those who were eagerly waiting to learn from the successes and failures of Promiseland.

What has happened in the last five years can only be classified as a "God thing." The annual Promiseland Conference on the Willow campus sells out months in advance and international conferences often attract larger numbers of people than our venues can accommodate. The Promiseland Curriculum is being used in thousands of churches and most of us sense that the rocket is just leaving the launching pad.

This book explains why Sue's ministry has catalyzed so many leaders who love and minister to kids. As you read it you will feel her optimism and catch her infectious enthusiasm. You will be reminded that kids matter to God and ought to matter more to us and to the church.

It has been a joy to serve alongside Sue for fifteen years. Her intensity and vision have sharpened my own, and her friendship has been invaluable to my wife and me. I wish you could spend an hour in a meeting with her, to see the sheer energy that infects everything she does. My hope is that this book gives you a window into the exciting world Sue and her team have created in Promiseland.

I join with Sue in dreaming of the day when every child is within a bike ride of a transforming children's ministry. Maybe you will become a part of the worldwide team that is committed to that revolution! To what greater purpose could you give your life and future?

Bill Hybels
Senior Pastor
Willow Creek Community Church

FOREWORD
BY GEORGE BARNA

For more than two decades I have been studying the beliefs and behavior of the American people. Examining a wide range of data drawn from more than six hundred national surveys we have conducted during that time, and focusing most closely on the intersection of faith, lifestyle, and culture, I have found that one disturbing result is incontestable: Christians, overall, do not behave much differently than non-Christians.

That is an odd discovery. After all, the basis of Christianity is transformation: we are to be so changed by our understanding of God's radical love for us and our commitment to obeying his commands and principles that our entire approach to life is redefined.

This indistinctiveness of the Christian community has troubled me for years, leading to a concerted effort to examine the problem more closely. What we have learned has startled me—and forever changed me. In a nutshell, we found that Christians do not act like Jesus because they do not think like Jesus. They do not think like him because nobody cared enough about their spiritual contours when they were young to intentionally and comprehensively train their minds to fully know, embrace, and carry out God's principles. In other words, few youngsters have had the privilege of having their worldview intentionally shaped to completely reflect foundational scriptural teachings.

The research findings revealed some astounding facts. For instance, did you know that the ideas driving people's behavior are generally acquired and adopted before a person reaches the age of thirteen? Were you aware that the religious beliefs a person develops by the age of thirteen are pretty much the set of beliefs they will maintain until they die? I was not. I was shocked to find how few instances of changes in belief occur during the teen and adult years. Further, we found that people's major spiritual choices are generally made when they are young, again underscoring the importance of focusing on the development of children.

Taking the research further, we then examined the process of spiritual development that occurs both in the home and in the church. Sadly, the results indicated that each party is waiting for the other to do the heavy lifting of spiritual teaching, providing feedback, and instituting accountability. While parents and churches tend to focus on their own survival and needs, children often get lost in the shuffle and suffer the consequences of benign spiritual neglect.

So the disturbing outcome—the absence of a compelling Christian witness to the non-Christian world—is merely proof of a biblical truth: You reap what you sow. Churches want kids to enjoy church so they will return as adults, because adult attendance is how we measure ministry success. Parents expect the church to inculcate spiritual thinking, behavior, experiences, and knowledge in the minds and hearts of their children because, after all, the church is the "expert" in that arena. But while each awaits the other's best efforts, our children are seduced and won over by the world through the alternative values and lifestyles presented by the media, schools, and peers.

It is not supposed to work this way. And, thankfully, in some churches and families across the nation, it doesn't. There are a number of healthy churches and Christian households with effective ministries to children that produce spiritual dynamos.

How do those churches and families facilitate such outcomes? That's what this book is all about. These pages represent a treasury of proven wisdom and insights into how to be used by the Holy Spirit to bring about exhilarating transformation in the lives of children. Drawing from the renowned Promiseland ministry at Willow Creek Community Church, this book will help you discover specific means to ushering in serious life-change among young people. Sue and David provide a highly readable and very practical guide to adopting the underlying principles that will create such a ministry in your church, too. You will learn about calling, leadership, creativity, chaos management, attitude development, evaluation, strategic thinking, recruiting volunteers, and much more.

During my time as a "Creeker" and in my many return visits to Willow Creek over the years, the energy, enthusiasm, and emphasis of the children's ministry never cease to impress me. Willow is a church that invests heavily in children because it is the right thing to do: these young ones matter deeply to God and represent the future of the Church and our world. I pray that you will get a sense of what your ministry to children can be like through exposure to the principles that have made Promiseland a life-transforming adventure. There is no ministry more worthy of huge investment than your outreach to children.

George Barna
Ventura, California
December 2003

INTRODUCTION

Sunday, 8:15 a.m. at Willow Creek Community Church

Promiseland is busy. No kids have arrived yet, but the team is here. Onstage in the large group room, two actors rehearse their lines. Over to the left I see Dennis leading a meeting with the second- and third-grade small group leaders. "Today's the big day because it's salvation message weekend," he says. They huddle together to pray for kids to choose to start a relationship with Jesus in the hour to come. His team—all volunteers—is filled with excitement because they know they'll lead life-changing discussions, and possibly witness redemption from only a few feet away. At this moment there's no place on the planet they'd rather be.

_8:58 a.m._

Promiseland is rocking. Children and adult leaders play side by side at activity stations. The sound of laughter mixed with clicking and clacking game pieces tells me the kids are glad to be here.

_9:03 a.m._

Small group leaders sit with their kids and ask a question designed to get everyone talking. A buzz fills the room from all the discussion and pent-up excitement—in children and in leaders.

_9:22 a.m._

After creatively explaining the gospel message, the large group teacher gives everyone the opportunity to ask Jesus to forgive his or her sins and be their forever friend. The stillness in a room packed with kids makes my heart race. The Holy Spirit is working right here, right now.

_9:30 a.m._

The band finishes their last song. The kids get up and run to the place their particular small group meets each week—the boys' Orange team here, girls' Blue team over there, and so on through the rainbow. The leaders start asking discussion-generating *questions. A group of ten boys who have just started attending sit together as the Gold team, led by a man gifted at shepherding new kids. Every child has a place where they feel they belong.*

10:05 a.m.

Parents arrive to pick up their kids. As third-grader Matt leaves with his father, his small group leader offers a parting comment: "Way to go, Matt!" Based on the leader's smile, I know what happened. Matt began a walk with Christ today. For the rest of his life, Matt will remember this hour and this place. And so will I.

Undeniable Change

"I just ask other kids if they are Christians," explains eight-year-old Jesse. "If they say no, then I tell them what a Christian is and ask them if they want to be one." Although this young evangelist is passionate about his work, he maintains a realistic ministry pace. "I do it on Monday, Wednesday, and Friday," he says. "And when I lead someone to Christ, then I take a day off."

Because it comes from a child, Jesse's perspective may seem simplistic or possibly even trite. Until you consider the results of his efforts. In one school year he helped eighteen schoolmates start a relationship with Jesus through a salvation prayer.

The children's ministry Jesse attends—TreeHouse Ministry at Rolling Hills Community Church in Portland, Oregon—helped to develop his spiritual roots and then continued to feed his passion for reaching other kids with God's truth and love. If you're thinking "Wow! What a powerful children's ministry that church must have," then you are exactly right. But that wasn't always so. Rolling Hills very deliberately transformed its kids' ministry to create this type of impact. While their old way of doing ministry involved Bible stories, these stories weren't creative and definitely not memorable. Jesse and others his age simply spent an hour in a classroom just like they did in school.

But today the Bible stories presented by gifted communicators come alive and make sense. Kids build relationships in small groups led by passionate shepherds like Mr. Jim and Ms. Brandy. Each week at TreeHouse Jesse learns a Bible lesson, discusses real-life applications of that lesson, and remembers it so well that he shares it with friends on the playground throughout the week. Starting with a message that prompted him to want a relationship with Jesus, Jesse knows that what he learns on Sunday can change others' lives throughout the week.

For several weeks, the pastor of North Tryon Presbyterian Church on Prince Edward Island, Canada, asked if anyone in the congregation of one hundred would be willing to lead their children's ministry. The previous director had left, and the children's ministry doors were to remain shut until someone stepped forward.

Paulette decided to be that someone. As a mother of four, she knew that her church must have a place for kids—especially her own. So she spoke with her senior pastor and offered to help. He gave her materials that described a new way to approach children's ministry—materials that sparked a passion in her to do it better than it had ever been done before.

She realized, though, that she couldn't do this new job alone. So she held an awareness meeting for all the church's adults. With only her kids to help, Paulette decided to give everyone a taste of the potential she envisioned for children's ministry. The game plan was to let the adults experience an exciting kids' program straight from the new curriculum the church had purchased. Each adult in the church received a personal invitation prepared by Paulette's four children. Attendance was good. The results were incredible.

Kids guided adults through activity tables while worship music for children filled the room. Everyone watched a video Bible lesson, then participated in additional activities. At the end of the session, Paulette addressed the adults for only a few minutes, saying, "This is what our children's ministry could be, and right now we're only missing one thing—you!" Kids stood by the doors with sign-up sheets, but never expected what would happen next.

From a church of one hundred adults, Paulette's children's ministry attracted sixty-one volunteers! The ministry grew to twenty-four kids in its first few months—and now children invite their friends to church. The new children's program has such strong appeal that Paulette continues to have adults ask if they can stay and help when they see what their kids experience. They can feel the passion that radiates from volunteers.

The impact of the children's ministry Jesse attends is unmistakable. The energy found in Paulette's children's ministry is unbelievable. The life-change in both is undeniable—and begs two questions. What is going on in these ministries? And can it happen in *your* church? The answer to the first question is found in the pages of this book. The answer to the second is "Absolutely!"

Making Your Children's Ministry the Best Hour of Every Kid's Week is a team journey meant for everyone in the ministry, not just the director. To that end, you will find a section of creative personal exercises and team experiences after the last chapter. These activities will help you transfer the key principles from the book into your ministry, and draw your team closer together along the way. And if you are not the person who leads the ministry, know that you can be a critically important agent of change—so engage the content of the book fully and see what God does.

Jesse's and Paulette's stories are two examples of what happens when a new vision ignites and is then fanned by the Holy Spirit. And just as the results from one lit match can be very disproportionate to the match's size, incredible impact can happen in children's ministries of any size. So whether you host twenty or two thousand kids each weekend, this book is for you.

My motivation to write this book is because of all God has done, and continues to do, in Promiseland and a growing number of other ministries around the world. I want something similar to happen in *every* church—including yours. So consider all the pages you'll read as a "matchbook" of sorts. My hope is that the concepts in this book will challenge you in ways that disrupt the status quo. That is sure to result in healthy friction. Friction will create a spark. Then that spark will produce flames. And then look out!

So now that you're warmed up, let's start the journey.

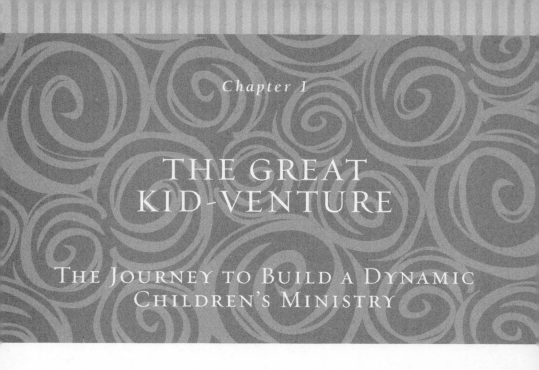

Chapter 1

THE GREAT KID-VENTURE

The Journey to Build a Dynamic Children's Ministry

An Adventure That Can Happen in Any Church

Children's ministry is an adventure, and I sure love adventure stories. There's just nothing like the quest to solve a complex problem, discover a lost treasure, or find a new cure. And the best part is watching the characters—how they're stretched and tested under impossible circumstances or unbeatable odds. It's fun to join them as they bravely face earthquakes, shipwrecks, or battles against stronger opponents. These stories require people's best, and then some.

And these tales have another universal trait—their creation. At some point, somewhere, someone pulled out a blank sheet of paper and began to write. Okay, maybe today they'd click to open a new document. The point is that someone deliberately decides to tell a tale that's never been told.

Including the stories that God authors. Rewind the ark story and we see Noah erase his current lifestyle, turning his new blank sheet into blueprints for a boat that will earn him mockery from the neighbors. Abraham was promised a new chapter in life that required a move, and expectantly looked at an empty page until he turned one hundred—a story that was also good for a few laughs. Before Moses' fiery encounters with Pharaoh, we read about his new beginning that started with a famous bush. Even Joseph's life story was deleted and started anew when he landed at the bottom of the well. And what a legend *that* story became.

This book is also about an exciting adventure. Let's call it the Great Kid-Venture. And this story can take place inside any local church of any size and in any country—because it's about leading and building a dynamic children's ministry. The kind of ministry that prevails over time, and that does so much more than simply survive week to week. One with a plot that involves leaders who wrestle with how to teach the Bible relevantly to children, brainstorm ways to care for adult volunteers, and concoct cutting-edge recruiting strategies. And one that includes other scenes like intense budget and facility negotiations, safety and security precautions, and new kids arriving every week (especially in the infant area!).

Sound familiar? With all the action required to serve kids well these days, no one in children's ministry is bored, that's for sure! But the best part of the story is that God unfolds this drama for more than pure entertainment. He has placed each of us in a ministry with the potential to change lives. And sifting through ideas about how to maximize this potential keeps every children's ministry leader awake at night. Or at least it should.

> It requires a modern-day leap of faith for someone in a local church to dare pull out a blank sheet of paper and change the way ministry is done.

In Hebrews 11 we see that the common thread of many great Bible characters is their faith-filled lives. Noah believed God had a reason behind the boat construction, so starting over was okay. Abraham remained steadfast in his faith, even when his wife did the chuckling. Moses took a little convincing, but eventually had faith to believe he was on a God-directed mission. And had Joseph given in or given up, which seemed much easier than remaining true to his faith in God, he would have become just another Joe.

Today's children's ministries share common ground with these biblical patriarchs—it requires a modern-day leap of faith for someone in a local church to dare pull out a blank sheet of paper and change the way ministry is done. In many settings, there are years or even decades of tradition standing guard against change. Or maybe there's apprehension to do anything outside of the denomination's program. It can seem ludicrous to start a ministry over or even to seriously rethink whether it really works—to whatever degree. Let's be real—children's ministry must happen every weekend, leaving little time for pondering change.

But maybe there's something just a little exciting at the thought of a new adventure in children's ministry. Maybe it can be a place that kids love so much that they actually *want* to attend each weekend. Maybe it's an experience they enjoy enough to invite their friends. This thought—this dream—quickens the pulse of many children's leaders and can become the heartbeat of an entire ministry. And the good news is that this isn't a fairy tale. Every year more kids' ministries throughout this country and around the world decide to try something new—and report the awakening of a new, exciting day.

Often these adventurous days come filled with very real challenges. Throughout my tenure in children's ministry, I've known what it's like to survive the lows and then hang on for the highs. I have felt overwhelmed with panic from a shortage of volunteers on weekends. But I've also seen God convince a man to change his schedule so he can build into a group of fifth-grade boys. I have labored under the weight of a commitment that Sundays will never bore kids. Yet I've also watched God inspire creative gospel messages that help usher kids across the line of faith. I have tasted the loneliness that sets in following church leadership's resistance toward change. And I've also received leaders' support to expand our budget and space, support that can only be attributed to God.

Across years of meeting with and challenging leaders to begin a new adventure within their children's ministries, many have asked me to tell the Promiseland story. Most are surprised and encouraged to discover that our blank-sheet-of-paper experiences happen over and over again—and that we remain a work in progress. The rest of this chapter describes our ministry's early journey and provides five faith-promises from God to hold on to when considering or experiencing change. Then chapter 2 focuses on a personal epiphany that landed me in Promiseland. The remainder of the book provides detailed guidance that, when adopted, will help you start your own Great Kid-Venture.

The Story of How Promiseland Began

As you read the next few pages, you will see that our story offers at least one scene that will strike familiarity with nearly any ministry. Look for one or more that relate closest to your situation. You will also see that Promiseland hasn't always been so promising. But it will become clear how God can use ordinary people in extraordinary ways and give them the adventure of a lifetime. And he can do the same in your ministry.

In the Beginning, There Was Nothing

The Promiseland story begins with the genesis of Willow Creek Community Church. A twenty-year-old college student named Bill Hybels attended a New Testament course taught by Dr. Gilbert Bilezekian. During this class, Dr. Bilezekian often spoke about the amazing church described in Acts 2. This was a church completely devoted to Jesus Christ—one in which people actively loved and cared for each other, shared all they had with those in need, took care of the poor, and met in homes where they enjoyed deep community. *"And the Lord added to their number daily those who were being saved"* (Acts 2:47). What a picture! Dr. Bilezekian loved to cast the vision for this type of church, and always concluded with a longing to see it happen again.

Sitting on the edge of his classroom seat was Bill Hybels, who loved to catch this vision. God placed a passion in Bill's heart so strong that he often went to his professor's office to talk more about what this modern-day church could be. Dr. Bilezekian recalls a conversation on his patio in May

1975, when Bill announced that he and his team were going to start a church.

"I nearly fell off my lawn chair," Dr. Bilezekian says, "but I discovered Bill was serious. We prayed, we thought, we strategized. And it was there, in my backyard, that Willow Creek was born."[1]

So Bill and a few of his friends decided to launch an Acts 2 church in Chicago's northwest suburbs. Each of them held tight to a conviction that God was calling them to turn irreligious people into fully devoted followers of Christ. Because of their passion for that mission, they invested all they had to turn this dream into reality. But they still fell short of enough rent money for the movie theater they planned to meet in each Sunday morning. So they sold tomatoes door-to-door, squeezing out enough profit to enable the new church to open its doors on October 12, 1975. This core group believed that God could make anything happen, so they began with no permanent facility, no salaries, no long-term strategy, and no seminary degrees.

Interestingly, their leap of faith also started with no children's ministry. But that would soon change.

Faith and Nothing Else

The brand-new Willow Creek Community Church had an obvious problem. Families did not want to attend a church that had no kids' program. To fill this ever-widening gap, Bill Hybels called Jo Kelly, a nineteen-year-old Trinity College student, and asked her to consider helping in the Sunday school area. Jo agreed to show up and lend a hand. She arrived to discover that "helping" meant she was in charge, because there were no other adults in the Sunday school area. A quick inventory also revealed that there were no toys, no curriculum, no volunteers, and no budget. Not even a blank sheet of paper. Not exactly an ideal time to accept a leadership role.

But Jo Kelly believed God had called her to this position, and that he was larger than all the challenges. So she uttered six frightening but faith-filled

> She uttered six fright-ening but faith-filled words: "God, you lead and I'll follow."

words: "God, you lead and I'll follow." Jo describes her experience as Promiseland's first official volunteer and ministry leader:

"Each week varied widely—sometimes we'd have five kids, and I also remember hitting a high of nearly fifty. We broke up into two groups—'readers' and 'nonreaders' is the best way to describe them. We were so limited by space and volunteers, and there was no way to provide care for babies, because the lobby of the theater was just too dirty and uncontrolled.

"I had lots of easy-to-teach lessons, short memory verses, songs, and simple crafts. We kept the message simple. I regularly had to clean up the floor of the lobby because it was full of leftover trash and popcorn from the night before. Eventually the stage crew made me room dividers that we set up in the corners to try to section off as rooms. I brought blankets to serve as a clean area for the kids to sit on and snuggle up in, because the lobby was so cold.

"Probably the hardest part was volunteers. By being involved with kids, they would not be able to attend the service. As we grew, I depended on a small group of willing adults whom I had to pull out of the service when we had really good numbers.

"Mine was not a glamorous ministry. But I knew the Lord wanted me there, so I was content."

Park on that thought for a moment. Despite floors littered with stale popcorn and Milk Duds, shivering kids, and no one to help, Jo was content.

Consider for a moment — do you ever stand still instead of stepping out in faith, because you don't feel qualified for the calling God is giving you? I do. Are you afraid you aren't smart enough, gifted enough, or strong enough for the assignment? Sometimes I am. Do you ever shrink back because you don't have a plan or the right equipment to move forward, yet you can't shake the fact that God is calling you to move forward anyway? I do. God knows all about days like that — times when fear's grip seems to wring out any possible contentment. He offers this promise: with faith in him, all things are possible (Matt. 19:26). He is smart enough, strong enough, and definitely has a plan.

Jo Kelly stared down seemingly impossible circumstances, somehow keeping her focus on her faith in God and the mission to which he had called her. When Jo looked around, there were plenty of reasons to fail. Such is the case in many churches. But, just as Jo exhibited, a strong faith in God and a belief that all things are possible can keep a leader from blinking. God's call transcends any ministry challenges.

A Contagious Calling

Jo Kelly built Willow Creek's children's ministry from nothing, but then graduated from college a couple of years later, married, and moved with her husband out of the area. The church now had enough money to afford another staff member, so Bill offered the position to Phil Miglioratti, a graduate student at Trinity Seminary and a Willow Creek volunteer. Phil was known for his passion to reach unchurched families and his heart to pastor kids.

Phil faced a defining moment. He could pursue different kingdom assignments—better positions more in line with his training—or this Willow Creek job. The latter offered only a tiny salary, no benefits (except the free popcorn and Milk Duds on the carpet), and an enormous load to shoulder. But Phil's prayers helped him discern that God was undeniably directing him to this ministry. So he said no to more attractive options and said yes to God's calling.

Clearly, there was a lot God wanted to do through this new children's ministry leader. The setting was still the movie theater lobby. The blankets were still in use. But attendance had grown to two hundred kids and fifty volunteers.

To start, the volunteer team named the ministry Promiseland, because they wanted it to be a loving place where kids could learn about God's promises. Phil also found time to write Promiseland's original curriculum.

His greatest contribution to Promiseland, though, was a vision for a new way to do children's ministry that eventually resulted in a whole new approach. Each Sunday began with a time for small groups of kids and a leader to get acquainted. Then all the kids gathered for Together Time, where Phil and key volunteers taught the day's lesson as creatively as they could. (Remember, there was no real budget yet.) For example, as a teacher told Bible stories, he or she would string illustrations on a clothesline, so kids could literally picture what they were hearing. Then back they went to small groups to discuss how to apply the lesson to real life. This format was quite a change from traditional Sunday school, where one teacher stands in front of a class as kids fill in a workbook.

> "Nothing—no lack of facilities or supplies—nothing was going to stop us from loving kids and presenting the Bible to them in creative ways each week!"

The Bible says that people will perish without vision (Prov. 29:18). In this case, the people thrived because of its presence. Phil challenged people to imagine a place where kids would hear the gospel message in a loving, positive environment. A setting where Bible lessons were creative and relevant to kids. An environment that would prevail even though there were no supplies to make it happen. All in a ministry of volunteers who believed God would provide exactly what they needed.

And God did provide. Phil's leadership solidified and energized Promiseland volunteers who shared a compelling vision and knew their mission. One team even made home visits to build relational bridges with parents! This driving commitment to the ministry is reflected in Phil's summary of what was taking place: "Nothing—no lack of facilities or supplies—nothing was going to stop us from loving kids and presenting the Bible to them in creative ways each week!"

The passion contained in that single sentence was contagious, because when a leader lives out the vision in front of volunteers, they will serve with passion, enthusiasm, and commitment. Phil was so sure of this ministry vision that he could invite others into it with him.

Consider for a moment — how clear and contagious is your ministry vision? I regularly check with God about ours, and he always seems willing to refresh my energy toward it. Too many leaders try to lead a ministry fueled by something other than the combustible conviction that comes from a God-directed vision. His promise is that he will provide all that's needed when a God-honoring vision is pursued (John 14:14) — this will surely radiate energy to everyone close by. Such a vision is the basic foundation on which to build a ministry.

Perseverance Requires People

Phil Miglioratti was one of several key staff members who left their jobs when our church went through a major upheaval, unrelated to Promiseland, in the late seventies. But God called another graduate student to our church, this time from Wheaton College. Andy Hartman described his response to Bill Hybels' employment offer this way: "Quite frankly, I had never thought about ministry to children. I asked Bill if I could 'join' the existing ministry as a volunteer for a few months to become familiar with it and was sold in just a few weeks. I went to work as the director from 1980 until 1984."

When he became director, Andy put his hand around a large and growing leadership baton. Attendance quadrupled. Volunteers more than doubled. During this time, Willow Creek moved out of the theater into a newly constructed facility. The new church building was great compared with the old theater lobby—but still could not accommodate the first year's growth to eight hundred kids. So twelve months later, plans began for the next building phase, amidst prayers pleading for creativity to deal with the swelling numbers.

Fortunately, God provided Andy solutions in the form of people. "I joined the most energized people [volunteers] already serving that I had ever been around," Andy recalls. "These people ate, slept, and drank kids' ministry, and their passion was intoxicating."

But ministry also started to become exhausting. Leadership demands, volunteer recruiting needs, and space issues piled up. The pace forced Promiseland to stop writing original curriculum and buy published products. However, the purchased curriculum proved too narrow and not as seeker-targeted as the rest of the church, so teams of volunteers had to meet monthly to adapt it.

How did Andy persevere through all of this? First, he made it a priority to ensure that gifted people were serving in the right places. And second, he placed a premium on building rich community for the volunteers. The ministry demands were high, but those serving rose together to meet them.

Consider for a moment — how is the volunteer energy in your ministry? Do your people serve in roles for which they are gifted, or are they simply filling open slots? Ministry fills up volunteers who serve in the right places; they leave each Sunday feeling energized rather than exhausted. Every ministry can take a large step to avoid volunteer burnout if the tasks each person is asked to do match up with who God made him or her to be, and when everyone feels like part of a community. His promise is that there is strength in working together (Eccl. 4:9 – 10, 12).

Also consider the benefits of a community environment. Even a short time for people to share the ups and downs of life, pray together, and just relate to each other goes a long way in drawing people together. A team that values doing ministry together is likely to stay intact. This is true because while people find it easy to walk away from routine tasks done alone, they have a tough time leaving a relational circle of brothers and sisters. Serving teams in children's ministry might be the only place some people will experience community.

> While people find it easy to walk away from routine tasks done alone, they have a tough time leaving a relational circle of brothers and sisters.

Under intense conditions, Promiseland not only persevered but also thrived. Andy proved that volunteers flourish when they are in the right spot for the right reason, with each other.

Growth Begets Chaos

Following graduation, God called Andy Hartman to a new vocational "right spot." The growth under Andy accelerated under the watch of Promiseland's next director, Bob Beaver. The number of infants through sixth-graders in Promiseland increased to twelve hundred. Every inch of existing Promiseland space was filled to capacity, so Bob acquired two large trailers as a temporary solution. For the first time in its nine-year adventure, Promiseland hired additional staff, adding six people to help calm the chaotic waters. But changes were rapid and plentiful, and new problems soon began to surface.

Inconsistency throughout the ministry started to take a toll. Some kids learned very introductory lessons, while other teaching was more advanced—which yielded many confused parents. Only a few groups experienced creative Bible lessons, while others received traditional materials. As a result, many kids labeled Promiseland "boring." Ugh! This was a big disconnect from what the ministry started out to be. And it left many volunteers disillusioned. Promiseland's vision seemed to blur. This confusion, combined with heavy workloads, quickly led to volunteer burnout.

Consider for a moment — does the chaos that seems to be standard issue in children's ministry today ever discourage you? It does me. But I believe God allows chaotic seasons in order to prepare a ministry for future changes. Remember his promise in Romans 8:28, "All things work together for good" (ESV). God is in control even when everything feels out of control.

The reason ministry impact continued back then was that, instead of making quick, knee-jerk decisions, Bob did a great job of letting God lead. Leaders often see a problem and go for an immediate fix, rather than looking for God's direction. There's a delicate balance between taking action and patiently working a process. Bob's leadership choices to deal with all the mounting variables, yet not try to overhaul the ministry, were the right ones. God was setting up Promiseland for something big—but it had to be in his timing.

Catalyze Change

Bob Beaver continued to follow God's direction by assuming a different Willow Creek leadership role. All but two administrative staff went elsewhere, too, so for a while Promiseland remained leaderless.

By this time, though, Promiseland had become strategic. The church's senior leaders considered children's ministry critical to Willow Creek's outreach efforts, and determined it could not afford to have it run with no one at the wheel. So in the absence of any obvious candidates, Don Cousins, the church's associate pastor, became the interim director. And not surprisingly, he was exactly the right person for the challenges ahead.

Don's leadership legacy in Promiseland can be broken down into three significant contributions. First, he assessed all areas of the ministry and determined that major change was needed. He did this by listening to volunteers to find all the places where the ministry was stuck—where entropy had set in, where confusion was prevalent, and where people felt discouraged. He sat with the creative programming and curriculum volunteers and took inventory of what worked well and what did not.

When the picture of Promiseland's realities gained focus, Don decided the time had finally arrived to send the whole ministry back to the drawing board. The ministry had to stay open every weekend, but now it also had the mandate to reinvent itself.

> The ministry had to stay open every weekend, but now it also had the mandate to reinvent itself.

Don didn't hesitate to start writing on a blank sheet. His second major contribution was to clarify Promiseland's mission statement and core values. He brought the new mission statement to other senior leaders at the church to assure alignment with the rest of Willow Creek. With the help of volunteers, he developed six core values that would guide how the ministry functioned each week. The discipline of soliciting input led to far greater buy-in.

Don's third key contribution was to write realistic staff and volunteer job descriptions that were in line with spiritual giftedness and abilities. This allowed leaders to position people in specialty areas to help accomplish the ministry's mission in a manner consistent with the core values. The hunt began for folks to write new curriculum, creatively teach Bible lessons, and shepherd kids in small groups.

As is true for any ministry leader, Don also had the responsibility to work with the financial decision makers to secure much-needed resources. He increased the paid staff from six to fifteen in an effort to create a sustainable ministry structure. And early on, he identified that one position in particular needed to be filled quickly—a leader for the creative programming and curriculum-writing areas.

So Don called a friend who was part of the original group that helped start the church and was now an elementary schoolteacher in Chattanooga. You guessed it—I was that teacher. And a towering woman of faith I proved to be, too.

Back then if God showed me a forty-day forecast of rain, I would have believed him and built whatever boat he wanted. If he lit up one of my shrubs and it burnt without dwindling, I would have trusted him and told Pharaoh anything that needed to be said. If God promised my husband that we were going to have a baby when I turned ninety—well, maybe I'll skip that one. Nonetheless, the rock-solid faith in God I thought I had, one that led me to try any new adventure—crumbled at crunch time. All I could muster in response to Don's offer was a squeaky, "I'll think about it and pray." All with a hope that he would forget to call me back.

Back at Willow Creek, the amount of change Don initiated in Promiseland was possible only because he was a seasoned leader bold enough to define reality and to do whatever it took to generate effective ministry. He never considered letting current circumstances dictate compromise or settling for ministry done "good enough."

Consider for a moment — if you are a ministry leader, are you willing to catalyze change even if you don't have the answer or the plan? What about big change — the kind that requires full faith that God will lead you in the right direction? Is there anything holding you back from making changes you know are needed? God's promise is that he definitely has plans for you (Jer. 29:11). So change is not a bad word!

Maybe it helps to picture that every ministry leader receives the leadership baton in one hand and a pencil and paper in the other. Sometimes it's a blank page, while other times it's partially filled in. Nobody is ever given a finished page because God continues to write his story in every church around the world. The important choice entrusted to a leader is whether to change a ministry or keep it the same.

Promiseland learned that we really could just set everything aside and make all the necessary changes. A bold leader named Don had to take the lead, though. And just when the new writing was getting good, leadership was placed into my trembling hands—and I had to decide what would happen next. I knew that without faith it is impossible to please God. Fortunately, that faith emerged when I noticed that he had already started to write the next few lines. In the next chapter I'll share with you what I saw.

Chapter 2

IMAGINE THE BEST HOUR

A COMPELLING VISION
MAKES ALL THE DIFFERENCE

Yes!

Those three letters, *Y–E–S*, pack incredible power. *Yes* opens doors, while *No* slams them shut. *Yes* steps into the world of possibility; *No* watches potential walk away. Although *No* delivers finality, *Yes* evokes excitement—and sometimes apprehension—for what lies ahead.

I was well aware of the consequences of *Yes* when I accepted Don Cousins' offer to join the Promiseland team in 1989. Yet it was an easy word to say after God painted a picture of children's ministry that I had never seen before and have not forgotten since—an image so striking that it became the fuel that still drives me and moves our ministry. It's a compelling vision that many other ministries have caught and used to cause change in their church, and it's the focus of this chapter. The best part of this vision is that it depicts children's ministry that can take place in any local church, including yours—and to start it simply requires one *Yes*.

Beginning with a No

Ironically, my story began with *No*, which God would show me was the wrong answer. In 1988, I lived in Chattanooga with my husband and two children, where I was completely enjoying my fifteenth year of elementary school teaching. Willow Creek Community Church was but a memory. I had been part of the original group that launched the ministry, but the church had gone through tumultuous times in 1979; hard enough times that several of us had decided to depart. I still had several good friends at the church, but my family was comfortably settled in Tennessee. At least that's how it felt until a phone call interrupted me from grading papers one evening and, as it ends up, disrupted my life.

Don Cousins, Willow Creek's associate pastor, was on the other end of the call. He and I were still good friends, so our initial conversation meandered through many corners of life. Then I asked him about the church.

As I mentioned in the previous chapter, Don was on a search to find a director for Promiseland's curriculum and creative programming area. He needed someone who knew kids, could catalyze change, and would strongly lead volunteers as the ministry headed in a new direction.

"Won't be easy finding someone to do all that," I said innocently, oblivious to why he had told me about this position. He chuckled as he burst my bubble of naïveté and confessed that during his prayers about whom to ask, God had brought my name to mind. He told me that the reason for his call was to ask if I might be willing to consider a new opportunity, to just pray and see if God was up to something, to—

"To add layers of clothing and move back to the land of cold, gray winters, for goodness sake?" I interrupted, before laughing at poor Don.

After spending several minutes to convince me this was not a joke, Don coaxed me into agreeing to consider it. So my husband, Rick, and I talked it over and invested several late nights in prayer. To help sort our thoughts and arrive at a decision, we listed the pros and cons of this somewhat ridiculous idea:

PROS

All personal

- The job was about kids—my greatest passion area.
- I still, deep down, loved Willow Creek and had many friends there.
- I would love working with Bill Hybels and Don Cousins again.

TOTAL SCORE: 3

CONS

Affect on Family

- We didn't want to leave our extended family.
- Our kids loved their schools and friends.
- The church we attended was great, and we were actively part of a community there.
- I loved to teach school and had fifteen years invested in my career.
- The pay would be less.
- There was no job waiting for my husband.

Subtotal: 6

- Chicago winters drag on for *nine* months.

TOTAL SCORE: 15

The simple math led to an easy decision—the answer was clearly *No*. What a relief that God had not called us to leave Chattanooga! But Don still did. He called a week later and patiently listened while I explained how we arrived at our response. He understood, but still extended an invitation for us to attend a new Willow Creek conference in February. Tagged onto this invitation was a favor; Don asked me to stay a few days after the conference to watch Promiseland in action and give him input. That seemed harmless to me, possibly even fun, so I said *Yes*. I didn't even notice the door of possibility start to crack open.

PROS 03
CONS 15

Ambushed By God

The only way to describe what happened on that harmless trip was that God ambushed us. During one conference session, he convinced Rick that we must reconsider the offer and trust him with our future. Chilling words to hear while a major snowstorm blanketed Chicago. And on Sunday, Don led me on a tour of Promiseland that would change my life.

We stood to one side of an entrance to watch as kids poured down the hallways eager to get to their rooms. *Wait, kids excited to be at church?* I thought. Several new families attended that weekend, which made my excitement level go up as I considered what was at stake for the next hour. *Will their kids want to return, or is this the last these people will be seen in church?* Volunteers were hard at work, but their workloads looked too heavy. Many tried to do everything—take attendance, talk to parents, teach the Bible story. I noticed weary eyes. *How much can these volunteers do before they burn out?*

The Bible lesson time gripped me so tight I thought I would pop. The same children who had earlier stormed through the hallways full of energy and excitement (and maybe a little sugar from breakfast), now sat with bored faces learning the Bible. I'm a teacher, so I know that no kid ever willingly chooses boredom. *How many of these kids come only because their parents make them?* Then I noticed the decor—or the lack of it. From floor to ceiling, the place looked gray and sterile, devoid of the color and imagination that appeals to a child. *If I think the place looks bland, what do the kids think?* Then as I walked from one plain room to another, something new and unexpected appeared.

God began to paint a vivid picture on the walls of my mind. For the first time, I began to imagine children's ministry as the best hour of every kid's week. And that vision forever changed the way I look at Promiseland.

When the best hour of the week is at stake, kids will drag their parents out of bed on Sunday morning and say, "Get up, we're going to church. I don't want to miss Promiseland (or *your* ministry's name) today!" Gifted communicators will creatively teach Bible lessons in a way that intrigues and engages children of all ages. Kids will hang on every word of stories, then talk about how to apply a biblical truth to their everyday lives. The learning experience will include drama, video, storyboards, fun activities, music children think is cool, and other creative components to help the Bible make sense.

When kids walk into the best hour, they see decor that is colorful, interesting, and bright. It's a place they know right away is just for them and where they belong—even if they've never been to church before. A place they want to invite their friends to. Yet no matter how many friends they have or don't have, it's a place where they will feel accepted and welcomed. *ENVIRONMENT*

The best hour has a small group of kids for every child to be part of, where it's safe to talk about absolutely anything. And regardless of how the rest of the world treats them, they will hear encouraging words—never any comments that devalue or discourage. Yes, kids will taste biblical community and find it so delicious that they'll ask for more! *RELATIONSHIP*

And best of all, this hour will make a profound difference in their lives. This hour will reach lost kids—those who don't know Jesus as their Savior. This hour will also teach all kids about how to become more Christlike—in child-appropriate ways. If done well, the best hour will impact the way they live the other 167 hours each week—and even change the rest of their lives.

The best hour will appeal to the volunteers too. They will serve in teams so each person owns only a small, very doable piece of the hour, and builds caring relationships with fellow servants along the way. Their responsibilities will

> If done well, the best hour will impact the way they live the other 167 hours each week—and even change the rest of their lives.

align with how they are gifted by God, so the hour will give them life, not drain their energy. Every one of them will understand how their role fits in the big picture of the church, and believe that reaching lost kids and teaching all

JOHN 10:10

kids makes a difference. Maybe volunteers will receive more than they give, making this the best hour of their week, too!

Sleep wasn't in the picture that night, because the vision for the best hour kept scrolling through my mind. Questions appeared, too. *How would this type of children's ministry impact the rest of the church? Is the best hour too lofty a goal? What would Jesus expect from a children's ministry?*

What Does Jesus Expect?

I need to "push the pause button" on this story for a moment because Jesus' expectations are worth exploring. In Matthew 19:14 Jesus says, "Let the little children come to me, and do not hinder them, for the kingdom of heaven belongs to such as these." Focus on the words "do not hinder them," because there are so many ways that children's ministries, although well intentioned, actually divert kids from Jesus. Throughout my tenure in ministry, I have labored with the question of how to not hinder kids. Fortunately the Bible has the answers, which can be grouped into the following three key guidelines.

1. See Kingdom Potential in Every Child

Kids can be hindered from coming close to Jesus if we don't recognize who is at stake—people! The Lord made kids, loves them, and died for them. He values every one of them, and validates that little people can have a big role in his kingdom.

Consider the story in John 6 when Jesus fed five thousand. Verse 9 provides a key detail—a boy offered his food to Jesus. The one who runs the whole world in his hand could have ushered forward a man or woman to donate a lunch. But Jesus took what a child had to offer and unleashed some serious kingdom potential.

A more recent story involves a Willow Creek family. Friends invited Jim and his, wife, Chris, to a Mother's Day church service, and their daughter Brianna went to Promiseland. Jim and Chris liked the service, but Brianna *loved* Promiseland. Over the weeks and months to follow, this second-grader's experience changed the lives of her entire family. Jim unapologetically admits, "We kept coming to church because Brianna enjoyed Promiseland so much. Our kids wanted to come to church more than we did." Eventually their whole family accepted Christ.

So which boys coming through the church doors might be willing to give all they have to Jesus, if someone would just give them the chance? Which girls can God use to reach entire families? The honest answer is, we don't know.

To see kingdom potential means believing every boy might someday serve Jesus. Seeing kingdom potential calls for trust that every girl could possibly affect the eternities of other people in her life. When every child is seen as bursting with kingdom potential, the urgency of children's ministry increases.

2. What We Do Really Matters

Any ministry sold out to this truth beams with joy and radiates life. When absent, though, lifelessness sets in and everything gets dull. And if a children's ministry is boring, kids won't want to return—a definite hindrance! How many families stop attending church because the struggle to get the kids to go isn't worth the effort?

What we do really matters because kids can become true Christ-followers. Acts 2:39 says, "The promise is for you and your *children* and for all who are far off" (emphasis added), so something very important is at stake every weekend—the life and eternity of every child.

> How many families stop attending church because the struggle to get the kids to go isn't worth the effort?

More churches are beginning to understand that to function well evangelistically, children's ministry must play a key role. Bill Hybels explains:

> Today I believe the single remaining common interest or entrance point for non-churched people into the life of the church is children. No matter how lost a guy is, he still usually loves his children. And no matter

how off track a woman is, she still has a soft place in her heart for her kids. This means we have a wide open door to almost every family in every community worldwide when we love and serve their children. If a kid comes home from a children's ministry and says, "I met some kids, I had fun and loved it, and I want to go back," most of the time a parent will say, "Okay" and then return to that church. From a strategic standpoint to reach families, it's a wise investment. There are church-wide benefits on all sides of a thriving children's ministry.

When a children's ministry believes that what it does really matters, there will be openness to try new approaches. All will realize that it's okay for ministry to look different to reach different people. Jesus proved this when he used a variety of methods—mountainside sermons, individual conversations, even a handful of spit and mud. He still uses all sorts of people to reach and teach others, as long as they believe what they do matters.

A children's ministry director sent me this story:

> I'm the children's director in California today, but my ministry began back in Chicago over twenty years ago. While in high school, a friend and I ran a bus route that picked up kids from a struggling neighborhood. Usually, we saw no real "fruit," but we kept at it for seven and a half years. Recently I received an e-mail from my friend, who had been in contact with Melanie, one of the little girls on our route.
>
> Melanie was a third-grader when she started taking our bus. Her mom was on welfare, her dad was in prison, and her family didn't show any signs of hope to ever rise above their circumstances. But Melanie sure did. She accepted Christ when she was young, became an active member of a great church, and has gone on several mission trips that have led to twenty-two other salvations. Melanie wanted to thank us for pouring our lives into her twenty years ago, and to tell us that she now works with youth every weekend. Melanie said she doesn't know where she would be if we had not served God.

Two high school students drove a bus because they believed that ministry to kids really matters. And previously lost kids like Melanie would say they were right. The value of reaching people while they are still young is validated in studies by George Barna, which quantify that the older a person gets, the less likely it is for him or her to start a relationship with Christ.[1]

So whether ministry involves popcorn and Milk Duds, two girls and a bus, or you and your volunteers, Jesus wants us to believe that ministry really matters.

Holding a crying baby matters. Sticking with a rambunctious small group of fourth-grade boys matters. Brainstorming creative ideas for a new kindergarten Christmas service matters. Dialing the phone a few more times

> **Jesus wants us to believe that ministry really matters.**

even when the recruiting is lousy matters. If we forget that it matters, the thorns and thistles of discouragement will slow us down on our path to reach kids. And even though we don't always see the plans God has for us, he still sees them (Jer. 29:11).

3. Become More Effective Every Year

In other words, push to get better, continuously improve, and expect to see more fruit. Ministry was never designed to stand still (a trait shared with kids!). Stagnation is a quick pathway to hinder children from Christ.

Jesus told us to strive for more than simply maintaining the status quo. His parables about talents (Matt. 25) and minas (Luke 19) reinforce that we should constantly look for ways to make more out of the ministry that's been entrusted to us. In both stories, several workers were each given something of value and then later asked to show what they accomplished with their portion. Those who increased their amount were affirmed and rewarded. Those who played it safe and tried nothing new were chastised.

The relationship to ministry is clear. Be creative. Take risks. Explore new ways to make more ministry happen. The world around us constantly changes, and children do too. Remember, change is not a bad word. An unresponsive kids' ministry is on a path toward obsolescence and irrelevance; it will actually become less effective in reaching real kids.

Just imagine one of the workers in either parable coming back with less than what was given at the start!

So we must constantly use new energy and fresh creativity to reach kids. "Big church" lessons, "big church" music, and even "big church" words are for big people, so children's ministry must be done in a way that is appropriate for little people. Even though ministry to kids looks very different than the rest of the church (and often occurs in the basement), it is *not* a lower level of ministry, especially when it's improving all the time.

This is not an easy guideline to follow; hard work is definitely required. Look at it as encouragement, though, not as avoiding punishment—because the reward of becoming more effective each year is far more than any pile of minas or talents! Second Corinthians 5:17 states that "if anyone is in Christ, he is a new creation." Belief that this verse applies to kids is fixed in my heart. If additional children can be transformed and begin a better life trajectory because ministry becomes more effective every year, then the hard work is a price worth paying.

It was visions of this particular investment opportunity that kept me awake that cold February night in 1989.

No Becomes *Yes*

A lot happened during that visit to Chicago. God assured my husband Rick that it was okay to leave Chattanooga. I saw a vision for what children's ministry could be. And Jesus' words to "not hinder" kids came through loud and clear. The only remaining downside was the blizzard. Snow eventually melts away, though. God's warm pull on my heart was there to stay.

So I said, *Yes!* Not just to a job, but to a vision. *Yes,* I want to help make Promiseland the best hour of every kid's week. *Yes,* I see kingdom potential in every child. *Yes,* I believe that children's ministry really does matter. And *Yes,* I'll do whatever it takes to become more effective every year. This *Yes* to what at first seemed a ridiculous idea meant I would start in my new role as Promiseland's creative programming director less than two months later on April 1, 1989. And in 1991 I would become the ministry's director.

A Challenge to Readers

At this point, you have an important decision to make. The rest of this book is about changing a children's ministry. Reading from this point forward requires willingness on your part to pull out your own blank sheet of paper. So will you keep reading? That means openness to consider change—maybe a little, maybe a lot—regardless of whether you are a director, teacher, or behind-the-scenes worker. Seeing kingdom potential in every child, belief that ministry to kids really matters, a commitment to become more effective every year—these beliefs won't just appear on their own. Each must be deliberately and prayerfully adopted.

In fact, to build a dynamic children's ministry, or to take steps toward that goal, doesn't *just* happen either. But when leaders decide that the story God wants to write in their ministry is too compelling to miss, too important to ignore, and too valuable to spend their life pursuing anything else, the best hour *will* happen. It might take awhile, maybe even years. But it always starts with the same faith-filled step—someone says *Yes!*

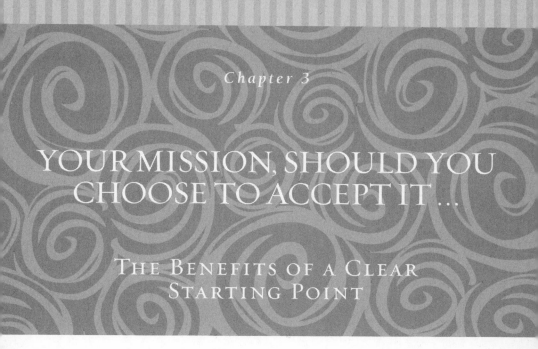

Chapter 3

YOUR MISSION, SHOULD YOU CHOOSE TO ACCEPT IT...

THE BENEFITS OF A CLEAR STARTING POINT

As part of the Johnson Space Center in Houston, Texas, NASA's Mission Control has the critical role of directing our country's journeys into outer space. Most people, including me, have never observed this high-tech control center firsthand. But millions of us made a virtual visit courtesy of the movie *Apollo 13* starring Tom Hanks—a film named for and depicting the true story of a spacecraft launch to the Moon.

> Mission is the grand purpose for which your ministry exists.
>
> *George Barna*

The crew of Apollo 13 blasted off from Florida in May 1970, confident they would land on the moon a few days later. Unfortunately, an oxygen tank explosion three days into their mission caused severe damage that made landing on the Moon impossible—and put the likelihood of returning to Earth in serious doubt. Mission Control, which intended to guide and support a trip to the Moon, was thrust in a new direction. Flight Director Gene Kranz, portrayed by Ed Harris in the movie, succinctly announced a change in their grand purpose: "Our new mission is to get our people home."

Later in the drama, we watch dozens of people in Mission Control—as well as a nation tuned in on television—agonize as the moment approaches when Apollo 13 tries to reenter Earth's atmosphere. Stakes are sky high—the ship will either burn up, bounce back into space to drift forever, or successfully splash down in the South Pacific. The camera catches Kranz as he overhears two executives whisper, "This could be the worst disaster NASA has ever experienced." Being the type of bold leader I love, he interjects a gritty alternative view. "With all due respect, sir," he says, "I believe this will be our finest hour!"[1]

Our Finest Hour

If Kranz's vision of the "finest hour" takes place, then NASA has accomplished its mission to get the astronauts home. When this obvious objective is realized, it can be seen as the end result of the mission. And, it seems to me, all of this has direct implications for children's ministry. A clear mission—one that leads to clear-cut results—is the starting point for making *any* children's ministry the best hour of every kid's week. Because when mission is stated well, everyone in and around the ministry knows what they will collectively strive to accomplish. Ignore or minimize the critical role of a thoughtfully articulated mission, and ministry will just bounce along, forever adrift. Get it right, though, and ministry potential knows no limits.

> A clear mission—one that leads to clear-cut results—is the starting point for making any children's ministry the best hour of every kid's week.

The bottom-line question is this: if the best hour (or even a decent hour) of a kid's week takes place in your ministry, what mission are you on track to accomplish? You needn't be a rocket scientist to answer that question, of course, because the Bible provides a clear definition—known as the Great Commission—of what such a mission should accomplish.

Will This Work with Kids?

In Matthew 28:19–20 Jesus says, "Therefore go and make disciples of all nations, baptizing them in the name of the Father and of the Son and of the Holy Spirit, and teaching them to obey everything I have commanded you." The mission he lays out is twofold: evangelize and disciple people. The "evangelize" part is easy to understand—we are to help people who are not Christians to enter into a personal relationship with God through Jesus Christ. But don't stop there, because that's only half the mission.

Matthew 22:37 reveals the breadth of the Great Commission's "obey everything I have commanded you." Jesus said the first and greatest commandment is "Love the Lord your God with all your heart and with all your strength and with all your mind." His all-encompassing perspective is obvious—there is nothing left after all my heart, all my strength, and all my mind are accounted for. In other words, Jesus asks for full devotion. So his direction to "disciple" people means that we are to help them become fully devoted followers.

But wait a minute. We're talking about kids in this book. Can we effectively evangelize kids? Well, most people will agree this can be done. But can children become fully devoted followers of Christ when their emotions (heart), bodies (strength), and intellect (mind) haven't yet fully developed? That undoubtedly seems a bit unrealistic—maybe wishful thinking at best—to many people.

But they're wrong. Kids can become fully devoted followers—they can indeed give their kid-sized hearts, strengths, and minds to Jesus. Child development expert Kay Kuzma asserts that childhood is the crucial window to the development of a person's soul.[2] And Karyn Henley, another expert in the field, agrees: "Children are more likely to exhibit a matter-of-fact faith in Jesus, than we adults who are skeptical of anything we can't experience with our five senses."[3]

Pollster George Barna quantified Henley's "more likely" description when he published data on the relationship of age to a person's likelihood to become a Christian. Between birth and age fourteen, he found there is a

32 percent chance an individual will accept Jesus. After that point, the number drops quickly to about 6 percent during the rest of a person's life.[4] This data compellingly shows that the chance of becoming a Christian diminishes with age. And I think the conclusion of all this is clear—the mission to both evangelize and disciple children is achievable *and* urgent!

Just ask Northcote Baptist Church in Auckland, New Zealand. Their children's ministry decided to get real serious about reaching kids with the gospel, rather than simply taking care of their little ones while parents went to church. One of the many changes the ministry made was teaching a new curriculum that clearly and creatively presented the gospel message along with a salvation prayer. Their director says, "For the first time ever, the kids heard the [salvation] message and we had ten kids out of fifty-five respond by praying for the first time!" This ministry now sees itself as being in the life-change business, not simply a diaper-changing service.

The Word *And*

For many ministries, the greatest challenge in their desire to "evangelize and disciple" is the word *and*. Some children's ministries demonstrate flat-out brilliance in reaching kids with the gospel, but then don't have energy left to grow them into fully devoted followers. Others do a great job of fostering the growth of the same five holy kids each week—but feel that reaching out to others will take them off task. They rely on new births alone to fill seats—so I guess their only growth strategy is more marriage enhancement weekend retreats! Even sadder are the ministries that strive toward neither objective, opting instead to provide convenient Sunday morning childcare and never daring to be anything more.

Reaching kids with the gospel and growing them up as disciples should be a dual mission, not a duel. The Bible doesn't offer us the option to choose one or the other—so our mission must include both. What does it look like in today's words? Let's sneak in to adult church and search for clues.

> **Reaching kids with the gospel and growing them up as disciples should be a dual mission, not a duel.**

The mission statement of Prestonwood Baptist Church in Texas says that they will "glorify God by introducing Jesus Christ as Lord to as many people as possible and to develop them in Christian living."[5] In Indiana, Grace Community Church's mission is "to love people into a responsive and maturing relationship with Jesus Christ."[6] The mission of Willow Creek Community Church is "to turn irreligious people into fully devoted followers of Christ." Although they state it in different words, all three churches offer examples of missions based on the Matthew 28 Great Commission.

So in Promiseland, we looked at the grand purpose of the church we are part of, and challenged ourselves to develop a complementary mission. Children's ministries should always align with their churches because they are part of an overall body designed to work together. Willow Creek's Senior Pastor Bill Hybels explains, "When Promiseland began to align its horsepower with the overall objectives of Willow Creek, and I saw all of the ways that our children's ministry was in stride with the goals and priorities of the entire church, I said, 'This is genius.'"[7]

But genius might be a bit too generous. We simply took what the rest of the church was doing and decided to do the same. To articulate what we should accomplish, Promiseland first acknowledged that we should help irreligious little people become fully devoted followers of Christ. However, just as everyone at NASA had a picture of what "get our people home" looked like, we had to consider the result of our mission—what does a fully devoted follower of Christ look like? And what about child-sized full devotion?

Five Indicators of Spiritual Maturity

Willow Creek describes full devotion using five key indicators of the spiritual maturity process. Each of these descriptors starts with the letter G: Grace, Growth, Groups, Gifts, and Good Stewardship. To successfully align with the church and to avoid the frustration of chasing an ambiguous mission, Promiseland had to put details and descriptors to the mission of turning children into fully devoted followers—in other words, 5-G kids.

Grace

In early December, second-grade students in a local public school were given the assignment to write about the best gift they ever received. All essays hung on a bulletin board for the month, including this one:

> The best gift I ever got was Jesus. He died for our sins. I got him when I was young. God gave it to me, he sent him to Earth. If I didn't have him life would be different. If he didn't die for our sins we would be died. I love Jesus so much!
>
> Scott

Every kid needs to understand Romans 3:23—that there is a gift of grace needed by all people. This understanding should include the fact that we receive forgiveness through a prayer of repentance and that we can ask Jesus to be with us to guide our lives. This fundamental of Christianity needs to come across clearly and relevantly to every kid, followed by an opportunity to respond.

Teaching and modeling that this free gift is to be shared with other kids who don't know about Jesus is also important. A children's ministry committed to developing the grace G in kids provides opportunities for child evangelism. No, I'm not talking about putting kids on street corners shouting the gospel at passersby. But opportunities exist every weekend when kids are encouraged to invite friends to church.

Special ministry events offer additional opportunities. One of Promiseland's successful efforts was called the Mega Sleepover, which we originally intended to be a relationship-building event for fourth- and fifth-grade children already in the ministry. When the kids heard there would be a band, cool activities, food, and very little sleep, their excitement grew. And grew. They began to talk about it at school. Then they asked if they could invite their friends. Soon, registrations climbed. They doubled. They tripled. Almost by accident, we had a can't-miss outreach event, now known as "Mega," for kids throughout the local community.

Fourth-grade Esther invited two friends to Mega, and they loved it so much that they asked to come back the very next weekend. So Esther's parents invited both families, and they accepted. After attending for a few months, both of Esther's friends accepted Christ's free gift of grace. Then Esther, both friends, and their whole small group started praying for the parents of the two girls to know Jesus. The eternal impact of just one sleepover event was, indeed, "mega"!

Imagine a generation of kids growing up expecting God to save people through the local church. Imagine an entire ministry full of kids who think that accepting Jesus as Lord and Savior is normal, as is encouraging friends to do the same. And imagine more second-graders willing to boldly describe to their school classmates the real "best gift ever."

Growth

After her bedtime prayer, a first-grader asked her dad, "Does God really want us to say 'sorry' for everything we do wrong?"

"Yes, he does," said Dad. "God sees everything we do, and is just waiting for us to tell him we're sorry."

"Wonder if we don't remember something; will he be mad if we forget something?" she asked.

"He knows we probably can't remember everything, but for what we do remember, God really wants us to tell him. Then he can help us not do that stuff anymore."

Long pause as her little mind races. "Daddy, I think I want to say another prayer."

Our kids' faith should cause them to change from the inside out—not because of a bunch of rules but because they want to. Children's ministries must simultaneously teach and model life as a Christ-follower, as described in Colossians 2:6 – 7: "Just as you received Christ Jesus as Lord, continue to live in him, rooted and built up in him, strengthened in the faith as you were taught, and overflowing with thankfulness."

I'm sure that most ministries share a desire to see kids grow spiritually. To assist in that process, two key elements of this G deserve special attention. First is the order in which growth is presented. Growth follows grace, just as living a Christ-centered life follows actually accepting Christ.

> **Our kids' faith should cause them to change from the inside out—not because of a bunch of rules but because they want to.**

Reverse the order, and a confusing life full of rules is the result, sure to repel any kid—or adult, for that matter.

The second element is the challenge faced when we try to observe this G in action. One clear indicator of children's spiritual growth is the stories parents share about their kids' changing lives. A commonsense filter is required, though. When a mother tells me that her son has stopped hitting his sister, it may or may not be a sign of something spiritual. If I hear that a boy is apologizing more for his mistakes after his class has discussed confession, then I get excited. (Although not hitting your sister is a good idea, no matter the motivation!)

When the right stories come in, the ministry is on course. If stories are nonexistent, the ministry needs change because impact is missing. A life that's lived more and more in Christ, even when it's kid-sized, is apparent to others. Parents can't help but notice improvements, small group leaders will see changes, and even friends will notice the difference. Additionally, this G includes developing a heart for worship, an interest in reading the Bible, and the desire to pray.

Groups

Fifth-grade girls' leader Roxanne describes small group life and her role this way, "Once relationships are built, they talk about a lot more than just church stuff. They look to each other and to me for advice. My goal is to inspire each girl to see herself more like the way God sees her."

Kids will thrive in a small group because it's a safe setting for spiritual growth to take place—and because it's true to the way we are designed. When God says, in Genesis 2:18, that it is not good for man to be alone, he indicates that he has made us to be relational people. In Mark 3:14,

> All people share a
> common need to feel
> connected.

Jesus forms his own small group—a ministry model highlighted again in Acts 2:46: "Every day they continued to meet together in the temple courts. They broke bread in their homes and ate together with glad and sincere hearts." All people share a common need to feel connected.

This need is abundantly present in kids too, for the exact same reasons. If a children's ministry can clear a well-worn path toward community, kids who attend are certain to better navigate the challenges of life they face now, as well as those that lie ahead.

After all, the world today is a heavy place in which to grow up. The disillusionment of fighting and war, the disbelief of abuse from adults, and the demands radiating from peer pressure all weigh on kids more than ever. And don't forget to pile on rising violence in schools while family time shrivels. All this means that many kids have no safe place in which to process life and build healthy relationships.

Promiseland offers small groups for every child starting at age two (more discussion on small groups follows in chapters 4 and 5), so kids grow up being part of a loving circle of friends. It is a risky gamble to assume that their relational needs will be met outside of ministry. It's a safer bet to count on leaders with a shepherd's heart, just like Roxanne.

Gifts

All Christians are given spiritual gifts that they are expected to use in the work of a local body of believers (1 Cor. 12). But expecting eight-year-olds to know exactly what their gifts are is a bit unrealistic. Children's ministries can, though, offer opportunities for kids to explore different gift areas and to observe adults in the church body model the use of their gifts.

For example, sixth-graders at First Evangelical Free Church in St. Louis, Missouri, had the opportunity to help build a full-scale rendering of the tabernacle (as described in Exodus) under the guidance of a volunteer named Mark, a professional carpenter.[8] Imagine the joy felt by those who love to work with their hands. My own children, Holly and Ryan, auditioned for the Promiseland kids' drama team as fourth-graders. They went on to receive years of talent coaching and life shepherding from our amazing drama director, Deanna. As a result, their stage skills blossomed while their characters grew.

I wish the church had given me these types of opportunities when I was a child. To me, there appeared to be just three ways to use a gift—preach, sing in the choir, or teach Sunday school. I never noticed the other areas of service, and no one bothered to point them out. I was oblivious to the fact that people with the gift of helps can make the church operate well, that administratively gifted people can keep the church organized, and that the gift of creative communication can make Bible stories come alive. Working in a church that places value on all spiritual gifts has educated me on the critical need for each part of the local church body to function well. And it's never too early to begin this education and valuing process.

Imagine the excitement for the church in a little person who wonders what part he or she will play someday. Or the open-ended anticipation in a kid who asks, "I wonder how God is going to use me?" or thinks, "Maybe one day I'll get to _____!" Of all the dreams a child will have about his or her future, I can't imagine a better one.

Good Stewardship

A family I know sat down one evening to discuss their church's expansion plans. The parents described how a larger church facility would mean more space to bring people who don't attend church and therefore don't know anything about Jesus. After looking at drawings of the new facility, the family brainstormed ideas to give money for the new building and landed on an idea that would encourage everyone's participation. They decided to put a large glass jar in their kitchen where everyone could deposit money—an activity that would serve as a visual reminder of their family's commitment to the church. As the family meeting ended, their four-year-old daughter jumped up and ran to her room, returned with her tiny purse, and poured the contents into the jar. When asked why she gave all the money she had, her matter-of-fact response was, "Everything we have is God's anyhow, right?"

The moral of the story is not that people must give every cent they have to the church. (Nor is it that if you do, you will receive recognition in a book about children's ministry!) The lesson here is that the basic foundation of good stewardship—everything we have belongs to God—can be learned at an early age. When people at any point in life understand this ultimate ownership, they will recognize that to manage and use resources wisely honors him. What a healthy perspective for a child to have in a world that encourages materialism and applauds debt! And while most children don't necessarily have a lot of money or stuff to manage yet, good stewardship also applies to a commodity they do have—time.

On Thursday nights our church provides food and shelter for area homeless people. Based on the prompting of small group leaders in Promiseland, we now periodically arrange opportunities for kids from our ministry to make sandwiches and decorate meal boxes for the guests. Kids on the Promiseland team work hard for a while, but at some point start to wonder why they're spending time packing bread and apples into boxes.

> Good stewardship also applies to a commodity children do have—time.

Then the kids see some of the visitors. Most times, there is at least one family with children the same age as our young volunteers. Picture hungry homeless kids thrilled to receive a bright box. There's always a long pause at that sight. And generally the same question at the end of the evening, "Can we do this again?"

Our kids begin to realize that even a small investment of their time honors God and can have impact on the people they serve. A child who learns there can be good uses and higher purposes for time and money is set up to succeed in the battle against greed and self-indulgence. And who wouldn't want that for kids?

Crafting a Mission Statement

Most people in children's ministry would agree that they aspire to nothing short of fully devoted followers—they've just never put words to it. Maybe it's called something else, but the clarity of results that comes from a description like the 5-Gs gives a ministry mission real traction. And once we knew the results we were after, Promiseland crafted a mission statement: "To supplement the family in reaching kids and helping them become fully devoted followers of Christ."

To understand the deliberateness behind each word, let's examine this mission statement one phrase at a time. *Supplement the family* clearly states that Promiseland is not a substitute for the family, because the Bible teaches that parents shoulder the primary responsibility for their kids' spiritual upbringing. Teaching that takes place in our church's adult service periodically reinforces this belief. In a weekend message, for instance, former teaching pastor John Ortberg focused on kids' spiritual development with these words: "Parents, do whatever you have to do . . . because getting your kids into a consistent pattern of Promiseland attendance and involvement is the best help that I think you can get with the most important parenting assignment you'll ever face."[9]

The rest of our mission statement follows Matthew 28. *Reaching kids* represents our passion to evangelize children so they clearly cross the line of faith. *Helping them become fully devoted followers of Christ* means we will disciple kids after they've crossed that line. We intentionally kept our mission statement short so that everyone can remember it. And although the logic behind it now seems simple, significant time was spent formally writing our mission—and every hour has proven well worth the effort.

Some people dismiss the need to write a mission statement as being too corporate for church work, or useful only in large churches. I've learned that a clear mission that is easily articulated and broadly agreed upon will deliver several benefits to any ministry, regardless of size or any other characteristic. We've already discussed an obvious deliverable—that everyone in the ministry knows what the group is collectively striving to achieve. But the benefit list is much longer than just this one.

For instance, I still remember several occasions early in my role as Promiseland director when new, very enticing ministry opportunities presented themselves—a common occurrence when a church experiences growth. It was my decision whether or not to pursue new ventures, and without a mission statement to guide my decisions, my nature would have nudged me to try whatever was new and exciting. Fortunately, I received wise counsel early on to stay on mission rather than to develop a "mission-plus" ministry. The fifteen words of our mission statement provided—and still provide—firm footing for deciding when to say yes and when to say no. And that sound guideline has spared Promiseland an untold amount of confusion and chaos. As you make decisions regarding your children's ministry, I would offer you the same counsel.

Several other benefits from having a clear mission statement also come to mind. For example, it will serve as a context to discuss your ministry with church leadership. When my senior pastor knows our mission, we can focus on progress rather than constantly explaining the big picture of what we are trying to do. This includes budget discussions and how money will be spent. In addition, the parents of our church know what to expect from children's ministry. And progress toward mission makes it easy for us to know what to celebrate with volunteers. Believe me, 5-G kids are worth celebrating!

Your Challenge

So how's your mission statement? Is it clear to you and church leadership? Can people remember it? Does it serve your ministry well by assisting in decision making? At the end of this book is an exercise you can use to either build or fine-tune your mission statement. Before you begin, though, give serious thought to mapping out success that is as specific as the 5-Gs. And don't forget the journey can only begin when everyone becomes real clear on what the core mission of ministry must be—to evangelize and disciple your kids.

Even though Ed Harris's profound statement in *Apollo 13* came in a flash, it might take more time than you think to articulate your mission. Relax—you're not in a movie, and the time invested will definitely be worth it. Remember that mission determines what your ministry will accomplish and is a prerequisite for planning how to do it. Because when your ministry's grand purpose is crafted well, then Sunday mornings will become your "finest hour."

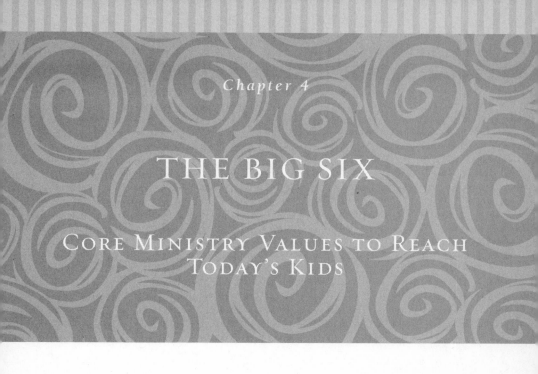

Chapter 4

THE BIG SIX

CORE MINISTRY VALUES TO REACH TODAY'S KIDS

I'm always amazed at the thoughts kids will share if they are asked. One weekend in Promiseland, hundreds of second- through fifth-graders completed a simple survey that asked them one question: "What is the most important question you think about right now?" If your kids were asked, what would they say?

We were surprised to find that 40 percent of the responses described some type of violence they see or experience—and another 40 percent struggled with various forms of institutional failure. Frequent questions included:

Why do my parents fight so much?

My brother/siblings/other kids pick on me. How do I make them stop?

Why do I get so mad?

Why does school have to be so confusing and scary?

My parents are getting a divorce—what am I supposed to do?

What is wrong with my family?

Why is it so hard being new in my school/neighborhood, just because I'm not cool?

One conclusion was clear; kids face complicated lives. So if Promiseland plans to deliver the best hour of every kid's week, we had better understand what happens during the other 167 hours. At first glance, children's weeks appear increasingly dismal. But keep looking. Because when we view life from a child's perspective, we find clear opportunities to more effectively reach kids. We just need to reflect their world in how we execute ministry every week. And that is accomplished when a children's ministry understands the world of their kids, and then deliberately develops core ministry values accordingly.

As you've already read, a mission represents the "what" a ministry does. But "what" becomes possible only when "how" exists in the form of well-thought-out ministry values. The need is universal—no matter what program strategy or structure is used, values dictate how we'll deliver ministry to kids.

In 1989 Promiseland had established no formal values. The result was inconsistent ministry. One week an incredible drama might engage the fourth- and fifth-grade kids, but the next week this same group might hear a story that seemed pointless and boring. One area would place an emphasis on creating a decor-rich, kid-friendly environment, while another was completely plain—making kids and parents think they must have stepped into the wrong room. Volunteers were not clear about what they should do because they didn't know what was important.

The ministry should have recognized this deficiency, but we didn't. We were fully focused on making sure Promiseland simply stayed in operation each weekend. We thought we didn't have time to deal with something strategic like values when supplies needed to be sourced, volunteers had to be found, and more kids were showing up every weekend. Predictably, the growing level of pain created by the inconsistency and confusion finally demanded attention.

So we set out to develop core, nonnegotiable values that every area would use. Fortunately, our associate pastor, Don Cousins, applied his seasoned leadership to this effort because establishing formal values was sure to introduce change to the way Promiseland functioned. And walking a large number of passionate people through change requires a strong leader.

Our team decided to build on top of Willow Creek's ten core values (see appendix B), and not to simply repeat the work already done. Through personal meetings, focus groups with key volunteers, and steadfast prayer, a large list of potential values emerged. We knew that trimming must happen.

Two criteria are essential for any list of values. First, keep only the values that guide ministry activity, rather than value statements that although true, are either too broad or too narrow. One example of too broad is, "We love kids." An example of too narrow might be, "We will use drama to relate to kids' lives." This statement demands drama every week! Picture the true feasibility of implementing each potential value. There is no sense in setting yourself up to fail based on self-imposed standards. The second criterion is that each value must represent the way ministry should happen when at its best. Don't set standards so low that ministry doesn't improve. Applying these criteria will result in a list of values that immediately become daily tools.

At every turn, we began to use our new list of just six values as filters for decisions. They proved effective. We continue to use those values in the same way today when we regularly ask the question, "Does this idea honor or violate one of our values?" As guides for the decisions and behaviors inside our ministry, values shape our culture. So much so that if I were to ask staff members or volunteers to name the Promiseland values, chances are strong that every person could do so. If not, I as the leader would own the responsibility to make that happen.

It's also a leader's responsibility to assign strength to these ministry values, and the best way to do that is to say no to opportunities that violate a value—no matter how attractive the opportunity seems and no matter who came up the idea. When a team hears that little, two-letter word, and understands the rationale behind it, they realize how committed everyone must be to the values. In addition a leader can strengthen a specific value by challenging a ministry with the question, "How can we get even better?" These discussions are a key leadership tool for any ministry that wants to improve.

I spoke with a children's ministry director recently who called for advice. "Our program is just stuck," she said, "and I'm out of ideas—what should I do?" I responded with a question of my own. "Sometimes it's wise to look at your core values individually for improvement, because that's where the heartbeat of your ministry resides," I said. "Let's go down your list of values—what are they?" The long moment of silence told us exactly where to start.

Unfortunately, way too many children's ministries operate with a gap because they have no formal values. Some have never found the time to develop their list because staying open from one weekend to the next seems like the only possible priority. Others have a list, somewhere, that seemed good at the time but was set aside for other urgent issues. Because ministry can happen without values, the gap often goes unnamed and unfilled. But the gap will eventually be felt.

> **Too many children's ministries operate with a gap because they have no formal values.**

If your ministry has a hole where values should be—for any reason— or if your existing values don't have the impact you think they should have, feel free to use the six Promiseland ministry values, and their descriptions that follow, in whatever way that makes sense for your ministry. Feel free to use them verbatim if you like, or modify them to your particular circumstances. A summary of values from additional children's ministries is listed at the end of this chapter to help with your thought process.

Value 1: Promiseland Is Child-Targeted

When Jane and her son Kevin walked into the church for the first time, they felt a bit overwhelmed. "Where are you taking me in this big place?" was the question going through Kevin's mind as they made their way to

Promiseland. After the service, Kevin had a new question, "Can we come back again?"

In order to accomplish our mission we look at every corner of Promiseland through the eyes of kids just like Kevin. As we do, we challenge ourselves with a variety of questions:

Are we doing the kinds of things children really enjoy?

Are we singing the style of songs children want to sing?

Are we teaching the lessons children will understand?

Would children invite lost friends here?

Honest answers to these questions will indicate how child-targeted a ministry is. To increase the "honesty factor," ask these very questions to volunteers, parents, and kids—and don't debate their answers.

Right now, you might be tempted to think, "We certainly are child-targeted because, duh, we are a children's ministry." Don't let yourself off that easy. I have a long list of things I've been told we should not do in Promiseland because adults might not like it. *Adults?* I suspect many children's ministry leaders receive pressure to please adult tastes. My response is, and yours can be too, "We have a place for the adults . . . it's called the morning service, and everything in it is for the adults—to minister to them on their terms. Promiseland is for kids!"

And because every children's ministry is for kids, deliberateness about our kids' activities is needed. Someone must constantly look for or write new music; give close examination to how long kids sit during a lesson; and look at the places children like to go for ideas on decor. This value, Child-Targeted, serves as a constant reason to consider change.

For instance, kids gave us low report card scores on music when we first adopted this value. They were adamant that our music was outdated. At first we didn't know what to do, because in 1989 not many real hot children's songs were available. We decided to ask our volunteers for help in putting together fresh music. We needed catchy music and lyrics, with cool motions, that made Bible truths learned on Sunday memorable Monday through Friday. That happens with pop music, so why not in Promiseland? Today a large number of our elementary-age kids regularly listen to CDs of tunes first learned during weekends at church.

One of my favorite songs, "Don't Forget,"[1] has become a regular in Promiseland's early childhood area. The melody is simple to pick up, the lyrics are easy for young kids, and the motions are irresistible. Imagine the impact on a three-year-old who remembers this chorus:

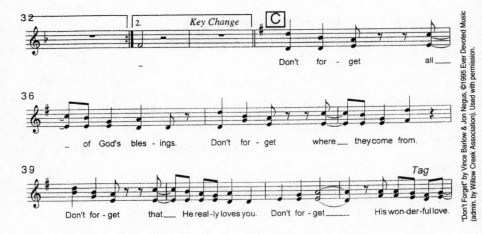

"Don't Forget" by Vince Barlow & Jon Negus, ©1995 Ever Devoted Music (admin. by Willow Creek Association). Used with permission.

Another challenging area is environment. Each weekend, Promiseland must convert plain, corporate-looking space into bright rooms with decor and furnishings that appeal to kids. And to do it all within a limited budget we have to be creative. During a ten-week camp theme, for example, small tents appeared in the hallways, as did signs warning, "Don't feed the bears!" Every week, three-year-olds enter their room by descending down a small slide. Four- and five-year-olds enter through a miniature door that's too small for an adult, but just right for a kid. Children see this and think, "This is for me!" And they're right.

Value 2: Promiseland Is Safe

I saw Barb in the hallway, and offered congratulations on her newborn baby. "I haven't brought her to Promiseland yet," she confessed, *"because I want to come in and just look around." I knew exactly what she meant—Barb wanted to make sure she was going to put her baby in a safe place.*

> Each weekend, Promiseland must convert plain, corporate-looking space into bright rooms with decor and furnishings that appeal to kids.

Watch your local news tonight or click on CNN for a few minutes and you'll hear our world described in many ways. But I guarantee "safe" will not be one of them. We want Promiseland to be a safe place for our children because it might be the only safe place they have. This value includes physical safety, emotional safety, and spiritual safety.

The world has become a scary place for children. Kids are very aware of school shootings, terrorist bombings, gangs in the halls, or bullies on the bus. And it's a rare day when newspapers lack an article about a child abducted by a stranger, abused by a parent, or sexually violated by, incredibly, a member of the clergy.

Physical safety can't be left to luck, and parents arrive at our ministry door expecting that Promiseland has done its homework. Parents naturally assume we have checked out the people watching their children. So we ask tough questions about everyone, yes everyone, in our ministry.

Children's ministries must take seriously the task of screening backgrounds for every single person—staff and volunteers—who comes on board. Making sure they are believers is a start, but a ministry must be able to vouch for the character of each person in the kids' rooms.

We have also ramped up our physical security measures. We constantly challenge ourselves to find ways to improve in a variety of processes including tagging/identification systems, establishing "no access" areas, and child protection training. Volunteers who work professionally in security can serve as a great resource for this work.

But physical safety is not enough, which I learned from an experience during my first year as a public school teacher. In the lounge two veteran teachers were discussing a particular child, using cynical remarks such as, "I don't know how much more of him I can take. Better hope he isn't in your class next year—you might want to consider early retirement!" I felt sick. *We're supposed to treasure kids like him, not belittle him. Isn't that why we are in this?* I thought to myself. I knew that this teacher's attitude was sure to be evident in her classroom, maybe very subtle, but it would show.

And it taught me a valuable lesson. While physical safety is often process-driven, *emotional safety* requires an entirely different mindset. Volunteers need to know that they are as likely to achieve emotional safety through tone and attitude as from a list of dos and don'ts. For example, we work with our volunteers to make sure that no child is ever told that he or she is a behavior problem. Our training spells out clearly that we don't label kids—meaning no one is stupid or lazy, a bother to anyone, or unwanted in Promiseland.

Volunteers must actively own this value. Kids want to see a smile—one that communicates delight that they showed up. A child's world might be upside down when they arrive on Sunday, so he or she might desperately need someone to act like "Jesus with skin on" to them.

Spiritual safety is also important. A volunteer shared the story of a second-grader named Jimmy who had spent his whole life in a wheelchair. Jimmy was unusually quiet through a lesson that focused on prayer. Finally he asked a question he had wondered about for years, "Why doesn't God answer *my* prayers?"

A spiritually safe place is one in which children can ask any question, or feel free to struggle with any tough issue. Let's not fool ourselves about this one—no matter what church you are in, there are children wrestling with very difficult stuff that has a spiritual aspect to it. For instance, what does a child do if her mom or dad hits or yells at her all the time yet claims to be a believer? When this girl hears that God is love, what does she do with that? What if a boy says that no one at school likes him? Or his dad says church is for wimps, but his mom says Jesus is a source of strength? What about the lost girl who says she doesn't believe in God?

> A child's world might be upside down when they arrive on Sunday, so he or she might desperately need someone to act like "Jesus with skin on" to them.

Such real-life situations convinced us that children's ministry must be a place where kids can struggle with tough life issues—ideally as part of being intentionally shepherded in a small group setting. And children's ministry must also be a place where they are never embarrassed. Sometimes this is as simple as stressing that nobody—big or little—ever makes fun of kids' questions.

Safety must be a core ministry value because even though Christianity offers the greatest lesson in the world, kids can't hear us when they are scared. Safety must be at a level so real that children can sit down knowing, "In this place nobody will yell or laugh at me. In this place nobody will take me that shouldn't. In this place nobody will do wrong things to my body." Kids must be able to say, "I am safe at my church."

Value 3: Promiseland Teaching Is Relevant and Application-Oriented

Katie invited her friend Abby to church. When Abby sat down for the Bible story, she felt more apprehension of her parents' impending divorce than intrigue toward a story of Jesus on a lake during a storm. She didn't even like boats. But then the teacher asked her and Katie to help tell the story by standing in the boat with several other disciples, and acting scared of the raging storm. The room was quite loud with the rest of the kids clapping their hands and stomping their feet in unison to mimic thunder and lightning. All went quiet, though, the moment Jesus declared, "Peace, be still!" Abby's interest began to pique when the teacher said, "You probably have things that feel like big storms in your life, but you don't need to be scared when Jesus is with you."

Everyone in children's ministry will agree that application-oriented teaching is important, but the real struggle is how to make teaching relevant. Didn't you struggle with the relevancy issue when you were a little person? Didn't you think the Bible was just for older people?

Children need to know that God gave us a book filled with wisdom to help them understand life today, and that his message provides unchanging truth they won't find anywhere else. Television only shows life they don't have. Video games come and go. Advertisers just want their money. God's Word is the same yesterday, today, and forever.

The pathway to honor Psalm 119:11

Children need to know that God gave us a book filled with wisdom to help them understand life today, and that his message provides unchanging truth they won't find anywhere else.

and help children hide God's Word in their hearts is to address the issue of relevancy. The goal is for kids to walk out of Sunday school and say, "Wow! The Bible is such a smart book. I didn't know the Bible could be written so long ago and still be so right for today!"

Relevant teaching starts in a simple area that is important to constantly test—language. Word selection, appropriate to age, is the clear pass/fail. If kids don't understand the verbiage used, the lesson is lost with no hope for application. Dr. Suzette Elgin says it best in her book, *The Gentle Art of Communicating with Kids*, "The only meaning a sequence of language has is that which the listener gives it."[2]

Obviously, the words a fifth-grader comprehends are much different than those of a five-year-old. And the Christian symbolism familiar to adult believers is foreign, if not goofy, to most kids. Ask young children if they want the blood of the Lamb to wash away their sins, and they'll think you're pretty gross. Tell kids that Jesus says he'll be in trouble for all the wrong stuff they do, and there's a strong chance for interest. Yes, words matter.

But word selection is just the start of relevant teaching. In Promiseland, we make sure three content questions are answered in every lesson. And (surprise!) the answers only count from the perspective of kids. The questions are:

1. *Know what?*
2. *So what?*
3. *Now what?*

Know what? refers to the Bible truth we plan to teach. This truth must be crystal clear so kids will remember it throughout their week. A key test is whether a particular age group can actually state the truth they've learned. Using the earlier story as an example, that statement might be *Jesus is all-powerful and can even calm storms.*

The answer to *So what?* is at the heart of relevancy. A bridge must be built to show that biblical truth applies to specific circumstances kids face; it can't be left up to them to construct the connection. Again, from our story, the *So what?* take-away message might be *I will face storms in my life, and Jesus wants me to know he can help me.* If the *So what?* question is addressed well, children will place value on the lesson. If the answer to this question wobbles, children will not care about the lesson. Let alone remember it.

Now what? refers to what kids are asked to do. Is there a clear and actionable application of this lesson in their lives? Don't leave the application up to their imagination, because on their own, kids won't necessarily think of *I should tell Jesus about the things that feel like big storms, and ask for his help.* The goal for each lesson should be to do everything possible to make sure that children "do not merely listen to the word" but "do what it says" (James 1:22).

Value 4: Promiseland Will Teach the Bible Creatively

Scott goes into action when he hears Dad say, "Time to go to church." Those words cue him to make sure nothing is still running downstairs. Video game controller power turned off. So is the television/multimedia center. Computer exited off that cool interactive Web site. Handheld game device rests in its recharger. The upstairs toys and the outdoor equipment are someone else's responsibility. "What will we do today in Promiseland?" Scott wonders as he jumps into the car, which already has the stereo tuned to Radio Disney.

This value focuses on delivery method. The need for ministry creativity grows as other sensory stimulation increases throughout the world for kids—television creates a high excitement expectation, video games offer

virtual adventure, and the media targets children with compelling messages. A dull Sunday school lesson, no matter how relevant, won't get children's attention; it will simply give them a reason to dread church.

This value surfaces a precarious question. I'm often asked, "Which comes first—creativity or the Bible?" I answer by pointing to the word order of this value. We want to *teach the Bible* first, and do it *creatively* second. However, they are not mutually exclusive—we can do both.

The solution is to apply creativity to teaching the Bible so that kids "get it" rather than "endure it." And to do so in ways that make them want to learn more. But the truth must be kept intact; a lesson can be so corny or funny that truth is lost. The constant challenge is to figure out how to make Bible lessons come alive for children, whether that means using a game show format, a competitive activity they play with adult leaders, or interactive storytelling.

> The solution is to apply creativity to teaching the Bible so that kids "get it" rather than "endure it."

Creativity used to be relatively easy when it was observation-based—a class just watched what happened in front—but those days are gone. Postmodern kids expect learning experiences in which they are active participants, not passive witnesses.

Aaron Reynolds, one of Promiseland's gifted large group teachers, tells the story of David and Goliath in a manner nothing short of brilliant. He invites ten people onstage and assigns them simple parts in the story. One person gets a helmet and plastic spear (or broom handle) and is asked to stand on a chair. You guessed it—Goliath. Another gets a shepherd's cap so he or she can represent David. Four kids receive plastic swords and stand behind Goliath as the Philistines. The remaining four take swords and stand near David as the Israelites. Keep in mind that none of these kids know what to do.

Then Aaron tells the story. Whenever he mentions the Philistines or Israelites, they wave their swords and jeer the other side. Whenever he mentions Goliath, the actor lets out an intimidating, "Hah, hah, hahhhhh!" (Well, as intimidating as an eight-year-old can muster!) When the moment arrives for David's stone to clobber Goliath, the actor playing the giant inevitably hams up his fall, the crowd roars, and quiet little David does an end-zone dance.

Once order is restored, Aaron looks directly at the children and reminds them that they will face big, giant problems, too. Maybe their parents are getting a divorce. Maybe they have to ride the bus for the first time, which can be a frightening thought for a kindergartner. Whatever it is, they can count on the same God that was standing with David to stand beside them, too. The lesson concludes with a challenge to pray very specifically when faced with troubles of any size.

I've witnessed the power of this interactive, creative approach in Promiseland's second- and third-grade room, as well as at a conference of a thousand children's ministry leaders in Brazil. No matter the audience, no matter the language, no matter the familiarity of the story, you can make the Bible come alive. And when it does, the truth God intended for everyone to learn is seared into the minds of those watching and listening.

On a few occasions I have asked a large roomful of children's ministry leaders what they remember most about their own Sunday school experience. The consistent answer is always one word—boring. But our God is not boring! Every church has volunteers—possibly high school students—bursting with creativity, who can develop lessons that make the Bible come alive. Go on a search for these people. It will be worth it!

Value 5: Promiseland Will Intentionally Shepherd in Small Groups

Tyler hasn't made many friends at school, so his eighth birthday is barely acknowledged by anyone other than his mom and sister. His dad moved out two years ago, and doesn't come around much. Tyler gets home from school and checks the mail. There's a card from one set of grandparents—the other set is always one day late. And then he opens a card from his small group leader, Mr. Phil, signed "Have a great day, Chief!" Tyler likes being called "Chief" by a grown-up guy, and feels just a little better that someone remembered his birthday.

Small groups serve as the perfect setting for adults to help children apply the day's Bible lesson to their lives and to connect them into community patterned after Acts 2. Both functions weave together and are critical to developing the 5-Gs in kids. Of course, the right curriculum is also an important ingredient to make this happen.

But sometimes churches can become so focused on teaching children information that adequate time is not spent on character transformation. My own Sunday school memory is of sitting down with a teacher in front of us, and spending the whole hour answering questions from a workbook. Nobody ever asked how I was doing, what was happening in my world, or if I was even doing any of the stuff we wrote in the workbook. Many of the kids in that class just drifted away over the years. Instead, children should make progress from year to year, meaning they should be more like Jesus this year than last, if application truly takes place. Only an intentional shepherd has a clear vantage point from which to observe such progress and to assure it happens.

Remember, though, that observation is two-way. When children are in the same small group every week with the same shepherd, they watch that person. The small group leader has both a privilege and responsibility to model a life committed to Jesus. Sometimes the small group leader might be the only Christian adult a child personally knows. To model effectively, these shepherds have a four-part responsibility to show up.

First, they must show up excited to be with kids. Consider the problem if children grow up in an environment where the workers in Sunday school always look disorganized or grumpy, and are clearly just doing their duty. Why would a child watching these adults ever want to grow up and be a Christ-follower?

Next, shepherds must show up ready to listen well. Much of a shepherd's tangible work is to make sure that kids understand the day's lesson—and to help them process out loud how they can apply it to their lives (the *Now what?*). This requires a strong commitment to listen. Unfortunately, many children have very few people that pay close attention when they talk. "My leader always has her listening ears on," four-year-old Erin says as she explains why she loves her Sunday morning small group.

Small group leaders also must arrange their schedules to physically show up every week. Promiseland makes clear to our shepherds that our ministry delivers community consistently; it is a nonnegotiable every week. Kids must be able to know people will be there when their life goes out of control. Consistency gives children something reliable, which leads to trust. Life's troubles tend to break the trust of kids a lot, so shepherds must re-earn trust every week.

Finally, shepherds must show up with an expectant spirit. The Bible repeatedly tells us to expect troubles in life, but nowhere does it say to deal with them alone. To that end, kids in small slices of community can see that Christianity does work in real people. And in this safe setting, they have the freedom to figure out how to really apply Bible truth to their lives, ask questions, and process life's ragged edges. Gifted shepherds thrive on this opportunity.

"I know we have real community when no one is seen as fat or thin, rich or poor, cool or outcast; everyone is accepted the way they are," describes Joy, a fifth-grade small group leader. "They don't get that level of acceptance in school or the neighborhood."

On Sunday morning, it is possible to offer a place to know and be known, love and be loved, serve and be served. It is possible to provide a place where every child is individually treasured and valued. A place where, every week, kids can build healthy bonds and trust with the same children and same leader. This place is rarely found in other parts of a kid's life.

> On Sunday morning, it is possible to offer a place to know and be known, love and be loved, serve and be served.

Value 6: Promiseland Is Fun!

Kayla scans Promiseland as her parents assure her they will return for her as soon as the big church service ends. She watches kids having fun at a variety of activity stations and thinks, "Seems good

79

so far. Nothing boring yet. A lot of kids are having a good time. Maybe this place will be okay."

The reason for this value is quite simple—kids won't come back willingly if it's not fun. And they certainly won't invite their friends. An absence of fun will result in an absence of kids.

Kids pay us one of their highest compliments when they say Promiseland is fun. This is a high value to us because children are more motivated to learn in a fun-filled environment. Let's be honest—you and I are more motivated to learn and serve when we're having fun, too!

I have good news about fun—it's easy to figure out! Here's our approach: Talk to parents about what kids like to do, and watch how kids play outside of church. Add surprises on Sundays because kids love surprises. Mix in celebrations. Physical activities are a must. Sprinkle in humor that they understand. We know immediately if we're hitting the fun value—smiles and bright eyes say it all.

Look for grown-up grins, too. When kids are having fun, adults will follow. And when creative elements are added to staff and volunteer team meetings, maybe a mystery game or generous amounts of chocolate (every adult involved in children's ministry likes chocolate!), the result is a spirit of community that keeps the team together and eager for future meetings. Fun is an allegiance that becomes the wonder of other ministries. Think for a moment, is there any other area of the church that can say they count fun as a core value?

> Is there any other area of the church that can say they count fun as a core value?

Walk through Promiseland during our Christmas services, and you'll see volunteer musicians and singers in the halls performing lively holiday songs for passersby. Check your child into Promiseland this weekend and he or she will start the hour at an activity area of his or her choice—possibly table games, crafts, or a competition. Sometimes we have hat weekend or a surprise party for small group leaders (spraying them with crazy string is totally optional). Over time, fun just becomes the attitude of the ministry.

Just as with all values, fun is used to guide the ministry in pursuit of its mission—fun itself is not the mission. When children truly enjoy their time in children's ministry, the environment is set for creative, relevant Bible teaching and life-changing, intentional shepherding. An important thing to keep in mind about the fun value is the danger in assuming that activities appealing to one age group will play well in others. Geography and demographics are important, too. Fun in Illinois might have subtle, yet important differences compared to what kids think is fun in California or Canada. (In fact, I'm certain fun is easier in California!)

A final thought about fun. When Promiseland gets this value right, kids start referring to the ministry as their own. And when I hear children describing what they do in Promiseland using the words "My church," my heart fills with affirmation that I am not crazy for what I do. I'm just having fun.

The six Promiseland values are as critical to us today as they were over a decade ago. They are timeless! And I'm convinced we will still be applying them for decades to come. I can't imagine ministry without them.

I have learned that effective values shine throughout a ministry. It's one thing to make them up and put them on paper, but that doesn't do any good. Values can become the bright light kids see when they look at a children's ministry, the warm light volunteers feel, the illuminating light parents understand, and the attractive light your senior pastor appreciates.

I don't know what your values are, of course, or whether those you have really work. But I do know it's worth extra meetings and staying up late at night to get your values done well. Only you can decide to invest the time to figure them out with the people God has placed on your team. Give it your best shot, because you're doing it for children facing complex lives and dealing with difficult questions. And when values reflect the world of kids, children's ministry delivers the answer.

Core Values from Other Children's Ministries

1. Christ-Centered
2. Kid-Targeted
3. Relational

4. Applicable
5. Safe
6. Fun

from Lois Waterton, Panorama Community Church

1. Creative
2. Relational
3. Application-Oriented

4. Fun
5. Transforming (spiritually)

from Michelle Dilmore, Heartland Community Church

1. Safe Place
2. Fun Place

3. Learning Place
4. Caring Place

from Lynn Magie, Essex Alliance Church

1. Love
2. Shepherding
3. Creativity
4. Life-change

5. Safety
6. Fun
7. Family

from Randy Blatz, Centre Street Church

1. Hands-On Activities
2. Exciting Fun
3. Age-Appropriate Lessons

4. Relationships
5. Teaching through Modeling
6. Safe in everything we do!

from Jeannette Cochran, Seneca Creek Community Church

1. God-Centered
2. Prayer
3. Excellence
4. Child-Targeted

5. Relevant Bible Teaching
6. Bible Community
7. Safety

from Brent Fink, Calvary Church

Chapter 5

LARGE GROUP, SMALL GROUPS, BIG PEOPLE

SO WHAT DOES SUNDAY MORNING LOOK LIKE?

Banana Bread

2-1/3 cups flour

1-2/3 cups sugar

1-1/4 cups mashed bananas
    (3 bananas)

2/3 cup shortening

2/3 cup buttermilk

3 eggs

1-1/4 tsp. baking soda

1 tsp. salt

Mix all the above. Grease and flour two bread pans. Bake in 350° oven for 45 minutes or until toothpick comes out clean. Makes two loaves of banana bread.

from the kitchen of: Pat Cimo, Associate Director of Promiseland

I admit that my cooking expertise is, at best, limited. But when I see a recipe like my friend and coworker Pat's, a few observations come to mind. To make this recipe you must want banana bread—not zucchini bread, corn bread, or any other bread. You must have all the ingredients listed, including the oven, or you'll end up with something other than banana bread. Then at some point you mix all the ingredients together and cook them. And after all your work, you must wait—full of anticipation for the moment when you eventually slice through the warm bread, savoring the aroma, and lift it to your mouth to take the first tasty bite.

What does all of this recipe talk have to do with children's ministry? Well, the fact that you've read this far in the book probably means that you want to dish up change in your ministry. You may even have worked on a clear mission statement and core values. These are all necessary ingredients for a children's ministry.

But the recipe requires more than mere ingredients. Directions for how to add, mix, and bake, are of utmost importance. Without these instructions, the ingredients just sit and do nothing. And don't forget that you need just the right amount of heat. To apply these principles, let's pull out a recipe proven to make a children's ministry really cook. Some people call this a ministry strategy—which is this chapter's focus, and is delivered in Promiseland every week compliments of hard-working, highly talented people like Pat Cimo.

Children's Ministry Strategy

one part Large Group
one part Small Groups
one part Gift-based Volunteerism

In Promiseland, three important components define our strategy—large groups, small groups, and gift-based volunteer placement. The three are dependent on each other, and don't produce much zest if used alone. But when mixed together, whether served in large or small portions, the outcome is gourmet.

Life Fellowship Church in Mt. Vernon, Texas, knows all about the difference a ministry strategy makes. Annette, director of their children's ministry, describes the impact of implementing a new children's ministry model: "We are a small church (twenty-five to thirty kids). As long as anyone can remember, we used a very traditional Sunday school program. When we took an honest look at the results, the impact on kids was little or none. Then we decided to try a new strategy—a large group/small group format and a new curriculum. Because of this strategic change, we routinely see several children saved and lots of life-change that is apparent to everyone. The impact of our ministry also spills over into the rest of the church. We have had kids who visited our ministry then brought their parents to church, and now the parents are part of our congregation. A new approach to ministry made a big difference."

Did you notice how our recipe above only lists ingredients? Still missing are step-by-step instructions on how to put everything together. If we examine a typical Promiseland service minute-by-minute, we can see exactly how the ministry is built around a large group, small groups, and gift-based volunteerism strategy. And a real close look at five specific blocks of time will show how the ministry's six core values are part of the mix.

Block One: Volunteer Team Huddles (forty-five minutes before start)

A volunteer team has set up rooms in advance, meaning all supplies, props, and microphones are in place. Small group leaders huddle with their leader, who is called a coach. During this time, the coach gives the small group leaders and other room volunteers the *VIP* treatment.

V stands for vision. Every week, coaches not only thank their volunteers but also remind them about the kingdom importance of their service. As I walk through the Promiseland hallways, I hear statements like "Kids are going to really understand what it means to have a relationship with Jesus today, and it couldn't happen without you!" Our coaches do a great job casting vision and motivating volunteers.

I is for information. The coach communicates any last-minute changes to the hour's lesson plan, which volunteers received earlier in the week. He or she also makes other important ministry announcements—perhaps about upcoming training, Promiseland special events, or even Willow Creek church-wide activities.

P represents the opportunity for huddle members to share prayer requests with their teammates. Volunteers who feel ministered to will have stronger hearts to care for kids. The huddle closes with prayer for the hour to come as well as for specific individual requests. The goal of *VIP* time is to connect volunteers with one another, share information,

> Volunteers who feel ministered to will have stronger hearts to care for kids.

and ensure they are set up to win. When adult teams experience community, they can then pass along that treasure to kids.

Core ministry value in place during huddles —
Intentional Shepherding for adults

Block Two: Activity Stations (thirty minutes before start)

A steady stream of parents starts to check their kids in to Promiseland a half hour before the service. At this point, each kid's experience in our ministry begins, and we want it to start well. As they walk in, children see several tables set up with a variety of games, crafts, and activities carefully selected to appeal to kids across a spectrum of interests. One table might have paper, beads, glue, string, and instructions for an art project. Another might hold tabletop hockey or wooden building blocks. A miniature basketball hoop might occupy a corner.

Activity stations change frequently to keep kids' experiences fresh, but this unstructured time consistently achieves two goals. The first is relationship building. Small group leaders find that these activities offer excellent opportunities to positively engage children with light conversation. "How did your week go?" is a question that can yield priceless information when asked by a gifted shepherd. Experience has shown us that kids usually answer that question more candidly while making a necklace or building a block tower, one-to-one with their leader. In this way our small group leaders learn volumes about their kids' worlds before the service begins. We like to think of it as "play with a purpose."

> The first impression children have of a children's ministry will determine their attitude for the next hour, so we want them to enjoy being with us from the start.

The second goal of activity stations is to create a fun-filled atmosphere. The first impression children have of a children's ministry will determine their attitude for the next hour, so we want them to enjoy being with us from the start. That includes new kids, who have an opportunity to fold in with the regular attendees through playing a fun game. And imagine the relief parents feel when they hear, "Wow, cool! See ya, Mom and Dad!"

Core ministry values in place during activity stations — Intentional Shepherding and Fun

 Block Three: Kid Connection (first ten minutes)

As the hour starts, music signals it's time to clean up the activity stations (yes, kids help). After a minute or two of everyone pitching in to pick up, children two years and older and their leaders gather into small groups for a time called Kid Connection. Everyone finds others whose name tags match the color of their own. Anyone new to Promiseland is part of the Gold Team—cleverly designated with gold name tags—until they establish a regular attendance pattern. Every child, though, has a group to be part of—a place to belong.

During this time, small group leaders ask kids one or more questions specifically designed to get them thinking about the topic that will be presented in the large group time that follows. For example, one week in second- and third-grade groups, leaders received these Kid Connection directions for a lesson about worship titled "God Is Eternal":[1]

WELCOME *the children to your group. Tell them you are glad they came today.*

SAY: *"Think of a time when someone said something kind about you. What did that person say? How did it make you feel?"*

SHARE *a time when someone said something kind about you [the leader], and how it made you feel.*

TELL *the kids, "It is always nice to have people say kind things about us. It makes us feel valued and special. Today in large group, we are going to learn about how we can tell God how wonderful he is and express our love to him. We call this worship. Listen to find out about different ways we can worship God."*

Kid Connection has two goals. The first is to help kids connect the week's topic to something familiar in their lives. The second is to warm up the group and make them comfortable with interaction. Leaders describe this as an opportune time for them to measure the overall relational temperature of the group before they meet later in the hour.

Core ministry values in place during Kid
Connection — Intentional Shepherding and
Relevant, Application-Oriented Teaching

Block Four: Large Group Time (next twenty minutes)

For their Bible story lesson, kids gather in age-specific rooms: those for two-year-olds, three-year-olds, four- and five-year-olds, kindergarteners and first-graders, second- and third-graders, fourth- and fifth-graders. We segment the ages into separate rooms since concepts appropriate for a fifth-grade intellect obviously differ than those designed for first-graders. In ministries where age divisions aren't feasible—due to facility limitations or a small number of kids—the teacher must develop deliberate wording and illustrations that span varied maturity levels and interests. It's not desirable, but is doable with a gifted teacher. A solid place to start age divisions is with all preschool ages in one large group and all school-age kids in another.

Creativity is unleashed during large group time in the form of drama, video, music, and other art forms that illustrate or reinforce a Bible story and show its relevancy to kids' worlds. An energetic teacher always leads large group time and explains the lesson with age-appropriate language. Lessons are designed to be interactive, engaging, and fun enough to keep kids' full attention.

Let's look again at the "God Is Eternal" second- and third-grade lesson referenced earlier. The Bible truth is "God is eternal," while the take-away message for the day is "God is the only one who has always existed and he is worthy of our praise." The teacher's script instructs him or her to welcome the kids, introduce and play a brief video, and then say:

"Our universe is a really big place, isn't it? It is amazing to know that God is the creator of that huge universe, and that he has always been around. The amazing thing is that the God of the universe wants to make contact with you and me. He wants to be part of our life every day. Over the past few weeks, we've learned that God knows all about us, that God is everywhere and we are never alone, and that God is king and in charge over all things. Today we are going to learn that God is eternal.

"'Eternal' is a pretty big word. . . ."

The goals of large group are to fully engage kids to learn and understand the day's story and to remember key truths from the pages of Scripture. The teacher challenges children with ideas on how to apply this truth to their lives. Anyone teaching during large group time is in a role reserved for only those who are truly gifted as up-front communicators—whether as a teacher, storyteller, actor, or musician. These people can create an environment of energy and fun so Bible stories come alive in ways that kids enjoy

> The goals of large group are to fully engage kids to learn and understand the day's story and to remember key truths from the pages of Scripture.

and remember. A boring Bible story presentation just isn't a palatable option!

Oftentimes large group ends with kid-appropriate music that reinforces the day's key concept and gives children the chance to worship God through song. When kids leave large group time, they have experienced a Bible story, understood a Bible truth, learned the take-away message for the day, and started to consider how they can apply this truth to their lives.

Core ministry values in place during large group —
Child-Targeted, Teach the Bible Creatively, and
Relevant, Application-Oriented Teaching

Block Five: Small Groups (final thirty minutes)

Children meet every week with the same leader and same six to ten kids during this time in the service. Just as in Kid Connection, children use name tag colors to find their groups. Starting in second grade, these kids stay together in their same groups from year to year, to the extent this is possible. A commitment to keep children with the same leader, and with each other, allows trust to build—a requirement of an emotionally and spiritually safe environment. But establishing a trusting, safe place isn't all we're after.

The primary goal of small group time is twofold. First, small groups are the ideal setting where we can intentionally shepherd kids—a core ministry value. Second, it is our chance to foster personal application of the day's Bible truth and key concept. In Promiseland, we accomplish this through a variety of methods—from games that pose lively questions to creative group activities that reinforce a biblical truth.

Perhaps you're wondering, "How does this actually work?" Let's revisit the "God Is Eternal" lesson one more time and look at the small group instructions. After asking questions about what took place during large group time to ensure that minds are engaged, the leader guides kids through an exercise. First, he or she reads aloud eight short verses that describe God from a variety of psalms. Then the leader describes the group's next activity:

SAY: *"Now you are going to have the opportunity to write your own psalm to God. As we learned in Large Group, a psalm can be a poem or a song that worships God. Your personal psalm will tell God how wonderful and great you think he is and include what you like most about him. After we are finished, you will have the opportunity to tell us about your psalm."*

The instructions continue with further details about the exercise. When the children have finished, the leader is asked to wrap up small group time with this:

TELL *the kids: "Today we learned that God is eternal, he has always existed, and he is worthy of our worship. We also learned different ways to worship God and had the opportunity to express our worship to God in a personal way. Take some time this week to think about all God is and worship him for those things."*

To close, the leader gives each child a Bible verse card, which helps kids remember the lesson throughout the week. Then the small group spends time praying with and for each other.

Promiseland pours a lot of effort into preparing our small group leaders for the big job they have—ongoing training and clearly printed weekly instructions are two examples. We want to keep their large responsibility as simple and focused as possible so that many people can do it. Because of their proximity to the kids, small group leaders probably play the largest role in impacting kids each weekend. Indeed when any child around our church is asked to describe Promiseland, the

> Because of their proximity to the kids, small group leaders probably play the largest role in impacting kids each weekend.

response invariably starts with words about his or her small group leader. Fortunately, the majority of people who step forward to serve in children's ministry have shepherds' hearts, so the role of small group leader fits them well. That's a gift and passion that comes straight from God.

Core ministry values in place during small groups —
Intentional Shepherding and Safe

Back to the Recipe — Gift-Based Volunteerism

The heat needed for ministry to succeed comes from people—because they provide the energy needed to make things happen. And as with any recipe, it's not simply a lot of heat that's needed—it's the right amount at the right time. Too much workload on too few people will result in burnout. And just like cooking in the kitchen at home, by the time my smoke detector wails the damage is done. On the other hand, too little work for too many people . . . will never happen, so don't worry about it! But do keep this in mind: ministries don't thrive because they have a lot of people—they succeed because the right people are in the right places. This idea comes straight from the Bible, most notably the entire chapter of 1 Corinthians 12 where Paul describes how a variety of spiritual gifts are given to people at God's discretion, with the intent that they will all work together as a church body.

When Promiseland launched in 1975, any volunteer was a welcome sight—remember, there were no big people to take care of the little people. But as the ministry matured and developed a vision, mission, and values, we needed to look at who was filling every role. The objective of this review was obvious—people should be performing tasks that are consistent with their spiritual giftedness. For example, only gifted

> Ministries don't thrive because they have a lot of people—they succeed because the right people are in the right places.

94

leaders should lead, only gifted shepherds should be trusted with a small group, only gifted vocalists should sing. Promiseland took, and continues to take, inventory of what spiritual gifts are needed for specific positions throughout the ministry and placed people accordingly. A list of spiritual gifts is located in appendix C.

A ministry must identify the spiritual giftedness of each person—staff and volunteers—to successfully place people in roles for which they are well suited. The result is realistic job descriptions that prevent people from burning out. Ideally, this identification happens when the person expresses interest, but prior to actual ministry involvement. However, and I imagine this is true for many ministries, we had to start by determining whether each person already serving in Promiseland had the gifts required for his or her position. When a mismatch became evident, a transition to a more appropriate role was needed. Now, moving forward, people are placed only in roles for which they have been gifted.

Moving volunteers and staff into new areas appropriate to their giftedness is never an easy process, but it is a critical one. Consider for a moment the result of people serving in the manner God has gifted them. The large group time bursts with energy and effective learning because the people in front of the kids are creative communicators or have the teaching gift. They radiate excitement while doing what they know God wants them to do. If stage sets or props are used, they look wonderful because a gifted craftsperson put his or her skills to use for kingdom work. Small group time excels because shepherds, not people simply thrust into that role, are doing the intentional shepherding. Those with administration gifts track and organize all that goes on in the ministry—with a spirit of joy. This is what God intended and what the Bible describes as all parts of the church body working together for his purposes: "Just as each of us has one body with many members, and these members do not all have the same function, so in Christ we who are many form one body, and each member belongs to all the others" (Rom. 12:4–5).

Those who put their spiritual gifts to work in ministry make an important heart shift—they offer a joy-filled sacrifice of time to God. In too many children's ministries, the driving force behind volunteerism is more guilt than God. Theresa, the children's ministry director at Living Hope Baptist Church in Bowling Green, Kentucky, found that most of her volunteers showed up out of a sense of duty. But when she changed her ministry strategy to a large group/small group model, she developed a drama team, technical team, props team, and a special events team, based on spiritual giftedness. She now describes her volunteers quite differently: "They are enthusiastic and consider it a calling, not a job. They know they can and do make a real difference!"

The idea of a gift-based staff and volunteer organization is applicable to ministries of any size. Fortunately, most people are given more than one spiritual gift, so they are equipped to do more than one task if volunteers aren't abundant. It is not uncommon for a creative communicator to also be a craftsman, a teacher to possess administrative gifts, or for a shepherd to be a leader. Of course, there occasionally will be times when someone must serve in a position that does not match his or her gifts. Some folks need time to explore and discover their giftedness. Just make sure this time of mismatched service is a season with an end date in sight, filled with prayers for God to send the right person. After all, serving in the church body according to giftedness—meaning everyone giving their best to kids—was his idea!

I believe many children's ministries find it easy to agree with the need for gift-based serving. Quite often the most practical challenge is to figure out how to start. When ministries ask me about this, I suggest they begin by recruiting a group called the "four sets of eyes."

Four Sets of Eyes

Any leader who tries to shoulder the entire load of his or her ministry is destined to collapse under the weight, especially in ministries with a new vision. So a good starting point is to establish a very small team of people, each of whom is a leader and owns responsibility for a different corner of the ministry.

	RESPONSIBILITIES	FIELD OF VISION
Overall leadership eyes	Makes sure the ministry stays on course with vision, mission, and values. Also must motivate, vision cast, and catalyze change	Entire ministry, focuses on anyone who leads a team
Operation eyes	Makes sure processes, policies, and people are in place so that the ministry functions well	Administrative and behind-the-scenes areas
Curriculum and programming eyes	Ensures that the teaching is effective and that kids learn and apply every lesson's key concepts	Content of large group time, small group time, and curriculum
Shepherd's eyes	Ensures the people, big and small, are intentionally and personally cared for, and constantly shares with others new learning on how to be a better shepherd	All kids' small groups and adult serving teams

We started with one team of four for the entire ministry. This team met regularly, brainstormed, and problem-solved weekend issues—and began to feel ownership of the ministry. As we grew and Promiseland became more complex, the need arose to either grow eyes on the back of our heads, develop X-ray vision to see in multiple rooms at once, or develop more groups of four. So we added one for the preschool area and one for kids in late childhood. Eventually, these teams replicated so that each room within the ministry benefited from its own four sets of eyes.

A Final Ingredient

Think back to the banana bread recipe at the beginning of this chapter—did you notice the missing key ingredient? To make the banana bread rise you must add 1-1/4 teaspoons of baking powder. Overlook this, and the banana bread just sits in the pan—and all you have is a hot banana brick. We also have one more ingredient to discuss that, combined with the other components, is necessary for children's ministry to work well.

Curriculum is an essential tool that coordinates large group time and small group discussions; keeps those gift-based, well-placed volunteers informed; and focuses ministry planning. For any given week during the ministry year, small group leaders should know in advance the key concept and Bible truth to be taught during large group time. Similarly, large group teachers should know how small group leaders will be helping kids apply the Bible truth in their lives. The weekly lessons of a curriculum provide the ability to preview and review virtually all activities for the children—and these processes are essential if a ministry is to be successful in reaching and teaching *all* kids.

Because Kids Are All Different

The large group/small group model delivers a mix of experiences to assure we reach the varied learning styles of children. In her book *Learning Styles,* Marlene LeFever describes a learning style as "the way in which a person sees or perceives things best and then processes or uses what has been seen."[2] In any hour of Promiseland, we strive to connect with every child's learning style in some way. But it doesn't happen by chance—we examine all large group and small group activities using a grid of educational principles that help us look deeper than just a curriculum's theme and creative presentation.

For example, we know that some kids are visual learners (seeing), some are auditory (hearing and saying), and others are kinesthetic (doing). Curriculum plans for each weekend must include activities to reach all three learning types. Child education expert Cynthia Tobias says, "No one is restricted to just one modality strength,"[3] so an added benefit of this approach is multiple points of connection with many children. Other principles on our grid include concrete versus abstract perception, and sequential versus random information ordering.

Moving kids between large group and small group settings and varying the activity within each setting means kids will never have to sit in one place too long. Of course the right mix of physical movement is age dependent and must be given as much attention as other educational principles. When we don't pay attention to how long we expect kids to sit, we often get it wrong. Careful review of curriculum from educational and common kid-sense perspectives helps us focus on the children, not just the content.

The educator in me instinctively knows that ministry effectiveness will be low when kids must sit in one spot for an hour and complete a workbook at the instruction of a teacher who tries to do it all. The message we have for kids is too important and deserves the best a church body can offer. Marlene LeFever says it well: "Christ gives us what we are to teach—the content—but the 'how' of teaching he leaves up to us. We must make the most of what we know about learning and the methods that communicate effectively with students."[4]

So *how* does this whole ministry recipe *really* come together? After years of doing my best to assemble the right ingredients, I've come to the steadfast conclusion that it all depends on who does the cooking. I can have the freshest vision and mission, just the right ministry values, and even turn up the heat of gifted volunteers—but only God can mix it all together well. Only he can make a ministry effective in reaching kids and turning them into fully devoted followers of Christ. So our job is to do our very best and then trust the results to the master chef. With that combination, the recipe turns out right every time.

Chapter 6

SHARING THE DREAM

GET WILD ABOUT VOLUNTEER RECRUITING

Baseball. It's America's favorite pastime—one that dominates the sports world for a full six months every year. Throughout America, many boys and girls want a piece of the action—a dream made possible through Little League. At six years old, my son Ryan was no exception. I'll tell you more about him later.

Little League teaches all aspects of baseball, and along the way makes it more than a simple game. Along with learning how to scoop up a ground ball using the hand wearing a glove or the difference between a force-out and a tag, kids learn the value of teamwork under the umbrella of sportsmanship. Parents also experience a wonderful learning opportunity, and I was no exception.

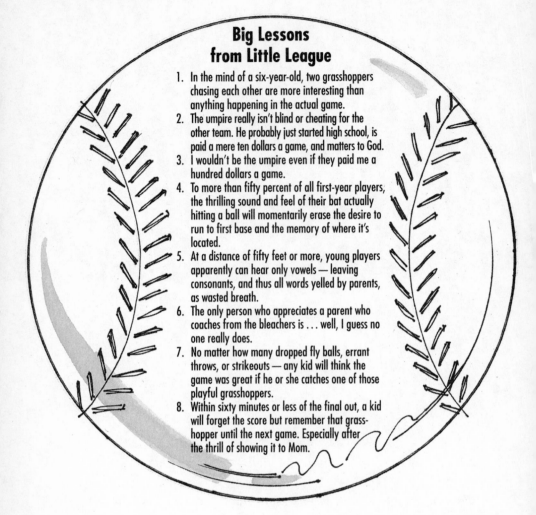

Big Lessons from Little League

1. In the mind of a six-year-old, two grasshoppers chasing each other are more interesting than anything happening in the actual game.
2. The umpire really isn't blind or cheating for the other team. He probably just started high school, is paid a mere ten dollars a game, and matters to God.
3. I wouldn't be the umpire even if they paid me a hundred dollars a game.
4. To more than fifty percent of all first-year players, the thrilling sound and feel of their bat actually hitting a ball will momentarily erase the desire to run to first base and the memory of where it's located.
5. At a distance of fifty feet or more, young players apparently can hear only vowels — leaving consonants, and thus all words yelled by parents, as wasted breath.
6. The only person who appreciates a parent who coaches from the bleachers is ... well, I guess no one really does.
7. No matter how many dropped fly balls, errant throws, or strikeouts — any kid will think the game was great if he or she catches one of those playful grasshoppers.
8. Within sixty minutes or less of the final out, a kid will forget the score but remember that grass-hopper until the next game. Especially after the thrill of showing it to Mom.

I also learned valuable *ministry* lessons from baseball. My son Ryan wanted to play in 1991, when a very unnerving trend was emerging in Promiseland. We had vision, mission, values, and a strategy. We were also in the midst of another growth wave. As the new director, my greatest concern was manpower. In volunteer circles, I constantly heard about gaps— more people were needed to make the ministry happen. Inevitably, or so it seemed, all heads would turn to me as if to say, "You're the leader, so do something!"

One big problem was that recruiting scared me. But I had to act, so I placed phone calls and gave people my very best sales pitch. But despite my sincerest pleas and even occasional tears, my batting average was miserable. I felt discouraged.

Then one day Ryan came home and said, "Mom, Dad, all the kids in the neighborhood are going to play baseball this summer. Can I play? Please, please, please?"

Of course we agreed. So we completed the paperwork, found out how much it cost, and attended the parents' information meeting. We looked forward to getting together with all the other families. We had heard that baseball parenting would be a big deal, and we didn't want to mess up. So we showed up early, anticipating a fairly boring presentation on league information and rules. What we experienced, though, was twenty minutes of the most motivational talk I have ever heard. I looked around the room, and every eye was riveted on this coach who was selling us baseball.

"Parents, this is going to be a life-changing experience for you and your kids," the coach proclaimed as he began to build energy. "This summer, your kids are going to learn sportsmanship. They're going to learn how to be good winners and good losers. They're going to be part of a TEAM! That means Together Everyone Achieves More! Parents, we're going to work together for a common goal, and we're going to partner in this for the benefit of your child."

I looked at my husband, whose expression left no doubt that he was wishing *he* could play. The coach was wild, and I mean wild, about baseball! Then he turned a key corner in his talk and said, "Parents, I have a few expectations of you. Would you please get out a piece of paper and write these things down?"

He said, "First of all, I'm going to deliver about eight boxes of candy to your house for you to sell. We all want to support the baseball program, and this will pay for its future."

I whispered to my husband, "Was this in the fine print on the application? How did we miss this part?"

The coach continued, so we had to pay attention. "Right now I'm passing out a schedule of the games and the practices. The kids will get hot, tired, and thirsty—so I want you to provide snacks. I would like juice boxes, in a cooler, delivered to the field. I want healthy snacks, not unhealthy snacks. And no glass; everything must be disposable. This will really help us partner together, so please sign up and let me know when you're available."

Rick and I started to choke. We knew one of us would have to remember to make this happen, and I was guessing it would be me. The coach closed by saying, "And finally, parents, we have these two Saturdays that are playoff days, and here's what I need you to do: choose a couple of hours to man the concession stand and sell refreshments, so that the baseball program can continue every summer."

I sat in my chair a bit bewildered. I remembered that we paid a registration fee to be part of this program, so the coach's requests seemed very bold. Then I looked around at the other parents, and saw that everyone was writing down every word this man said, without any questions as to whether they would do it. And FYI, everybody—including Rick and me—did do everything he asked that season.

Ministry Lessons from Summer Baseball

I learned two major ministry lessons from baseball that summer. First, God gently taught me that I didn't need to be afraid to ask parents to step up as partners in laying down a spiritual foundation for their kids. The baseball coach never said, "Parents, I know you're busy and I care about that." Or, "I know this is a lot to ask, and if you don't want to do it all, I'm okay with that." He just expected us to step up because these were our kids who wanted to play baseball. And we could see the benefits of what he and the program would provide them.

The second thing God taught me was that if I wanted to recruit others into children's ministry, then I must be as wild about my vision for children's ministry as this coach was about playing baseball.

Sure, baseball is a great game, and during that summer Ryan developed skills, was on an amazing team, and played for a fabulous coach. I learned some lessons myself. But I kept it in perspective because baseball is just a game—and ministry is about real life. I had to ask myself if I was as wild about changing kids' eternities as this coach was about baseball. Paul said in Philippians 1:21, "For to me, to live is Christ." When I personalize that statement, it means that my heart beats fast to introduce kids to Jesus and help them grow into full devotion, and to make children's ministry the best hour of every kid's week. My pulse races at the thought of helping a child arrive at the spot where he or she says, "For to me, to live is Christ."

I'm even wilder about it today than I was in 1989, because I can see how powerful life-change from Christ has been in the lives of kids. Are you wild about your vision and values? What about seeing life-change in kids or volunteers? I've learned these are important questions because if my passion about my ministry is anything less than obvious, then it will be difficult to recruit and keep someone longer than one season.

Because of my experience as a Little League mom, I realized that my approach to volunteer recruiting was completely wrong. I had been trying to recruit people to a need—not to a vision I was wild about. Tasks needed to be done, so I called to sign up people for an assignment. It dawned on me that I should say words like, "I want to partner with you in bringing a new day to our children's ministry, and let me tell you how your kids will benefit from it." But that was only one piece of a much larger game plan.

Elements in a Vision for Volunteers

To be effective, we must create a customized vision for children's ministry for every single volunteer we hope to recruit. It should be easy to understand because it's not too long or too short. A dream should be not so big that it seems impossible, but not so

> To be effective, we must create a customized vision for children's ministry for every single volunteer we hope to recruit.

small that it's trivial. Like a comfortable pair of shoes, the vision must fit each person just right.

A vision will fit just right when three elements are in place. First, *make the message significant to the listener's heart*. An appeal to sign up for a job that meets a need doesn't make an emotional connection. It might make sense to me because I know how the task will move the ministry forward. But to the potential volunteer it will just seem like a request to put in some time.

And people don't want to indiscriminately use or waste their time at church—or anywhere else for that matter. They want to give their lives and their volunteer time to something with purpose and significance. Everyone wants to do something important. Ephesians 2:10 says that God designed us that way: "We are God's workmanship, created in Christ Jesus to do good works, which God prepared in advance for us to do." Cinda from Valleybrook Church in Eau Claire, Wisconsin, knows how recruiting efforts benefit from such significance. "Our ministry did the weekend service and explained why we value children at our church. Then we offered people the opportunity to make a significant difference in the lives of children by inviting them onto our team. Close to seventy people responded!"

The second element of a vision that fits just right is to *show people how they can fit* in your ministry. Imagine that they're a puzzle piece. They have unique life experiences. They have different spiritual gifts. So show them how they fit into the whole picture of children's ministry. When volunteers understand that there is a specific place waiting for them—a place that's made to fit the way they are made—then they're more likely to step into ministry.

The third element of vision casting is to *make the time fit*. A mistake that I made early in my recruiting efforts was to ask everybody to sign up for an hour a week for forty-two weeks. You can probably imagine my strike-out average—it was high. So we changed our approach and offered a variety of time commitment levels to new volunteers. Promiseland's point person for recruiting, "fearless" Jim Braniff, now tells people, "If you have very little time, you can help us out. If you have just a few minutes of time, you can help us out. If you have rotational time available on your calendar, you can help us out."

With leadership creativity and solid coordination by gifted administrators, any time a volunteer can offer fits in children's ministry. This approach supports a goal to never turn away a new volunteer.

The three elements of a vision that fits just right are a good start. The next step is to consider *how* to cast vision and to *whom*.

Whom should we recruit? The congregation. Yes, the whole congregation! Don't worry, every person in your church won't respond, of course, or even qualify to work in children's ministry (remember Safe as a core ministry value).

To accomplish this tall order, layer the vision and present it differently, depending on the audience. I've learned that the same script doesn't fit all people or all purposes. Different individuals need to hear different messages, based on their proximity to or involvement in the ministry. Typically, there are five groups to consider.

Everyone

About once a year, the entire church body needs to get a glimpse of the children's ministry vision. Think of it as a broadcast vision because the audience is anyone listening and watching. And just like a media news broadcast, the purpose is to keep everyone informed. Specifically, there are two things a church body should always be aware of with respect to their church's children's ministry.

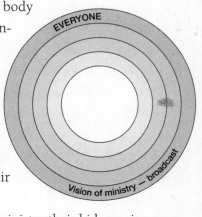

First, parents need to know about the ministry their kids receive every week. Time devoted in a weekend or midweek service to show parents that there's an awesome, rocking children's ministry in the building will help build a sense of partnership by showcasing one of the partners.

Promiseland views this as an absolute necessity—and a strong reinforcement of the first four words of our mission statement, *"To supplement the family."*

The other important role of a broadcast vision is to position the children's ministry as a tool to accomplish the church's mission. For example, everyone who attends Willow Creek should have confidence that when they bring unchurched neighbors to church, the children of those neighbors will experience an amazing hour in Promiseland. Imagine the evangelistic impact when attenders say to their friends, "I'm sure your kids will like it—Promiseland is the best hour of every kid's week." Who wouldn't want to try, at least once, to bring their children to what might be the best hour of their week?

Taking over part or all of a weekend service won't happen overnight, though. It took us years to convince our senior pastor that he could trust us with just five or ten minutes—because in Promiseland's early days, those moments had usually come across as so childish that the message was lost. But he didn't give up on us, and even issued a challenge for us to "put your best stuff up." So each year we determine which large group program from the past year was the most creative and effective. Because we want to give the congregation a real taste of Promiseland, we typically take a large group lesson straight from our curriculum and teach it to big church.

To watch the whole congregation acknowledge and appreciate your ministry is a sight that's tough to forget. And the reinforcing value it gives volunteers is priceless. In churches where children's ministry hasn't broadcast their vision yet, that day won't arrive on its own—so there are interim steps you can take to bring that moment closer. Invite your senior pastor or program director to a rehearsal and show them the possibility. Take just two minutes in front of the congregation if they'll give it to you. Make sure to clearly describe the church-wide benefits of broadcast vision to senior leaders, and include your pledge to do it well.

Lori from West Springs Church in St. Louis, Missouri, is quite specific about her commitment to her ministry's annual opportunity in front of the whole church. "Our presentation to the congregation must be kingdom-promoting, breathtaking, creative, well-rehearsed, informative, concise, full of vision and enthusiasm, sincere, and fun! We figure we have one shot to capture the hearts of the congregation with the vision for our ministry, so nothing mediocre or unprepared will do. This doesn't mean it has to be expensive, though. We have a very small budget, so we put our heads together to make a 'silk purse from a sow's ear.' It usually gets a high number of responses that kick-start our recruiting."

Lori's last sentence is important—her team's brief time in front of the congregation has the obvious benefit of being an excellent recruiting tool. Whether you influence it or not, most of the people in your church have formed a perception of your ministry—one that either helps or hurts your volunteer recruiting efforts throughout the whole year. The stakes are high with broadcast vision, and worth every hour spent in preparation to do it well.

Special Event Volunteers

All churches have people with a general passion to help serve anywhere in the church, especially at holidays or when other circumstances create a great need. These folks have hearts to help but may not be ready to commit to ongoing volunteer service. Promiseland has a vision and a valuable role for this type of person because, remember, we don't turn away any volunteer.

Everyone

SPECIAL EVENT VOLUNTEERS

Vision that service helps church

For example, we give our faithful, regular volunteers the chance to take ten weeks off from late June to September. That creates a big need each year for replacement volunteers, so we time an appeal to the church body for summer help right after a spring broadcast vision opportunity. This vision cast targets people who are willing to consider a unique and significant opportunity—serving as a special event volunteer.

Every May we say to our congregation, "We need to let our volunteers have some downtime. They've had forty-two weeks with the kids, and they need a little time to refuel. So each week we need some of you to help us. This will serve the whole church by letting our regular volunteers rest and keeping the doors of Promiseland open—especially for families who will visit Willow Creek this summer. You might hold a baby, sing fun songs, or sit with a small group of kids and listen to a Bible story. Whatever it is, you can be the hands, feet, and hearts that cover our rooms for an hour this summer until our volunteers come back. And here's your next step...."

1:6 Adult Volunteers

Let's move one layer of commitment deeper and communicate with individuals—specifically, parents. Remember my story of the baseball coach who looked at us and, in essence, said: "Hey, people, these are your kids. Step up." I don't suggest using that wording, but the spirit of what he said is relevant. Promiseland approaches parents periodically and says, "We've noticed that you've been attending our church regularly. How are you enjoying it? We've created a special opportunity for you to invest time in your child's room...."

Everyone
Special Event Volunteers
1:6 ADULT VOLUNTEERS

Vision for a role in this ministry

Although a parent usually isn't ready at this point to take on responsibility for a large number of kids, he or she will reason, "My kid matters to me, so I'll help." The significant vision piece that appeals to parents is their own children. That's why I became involved in the baseball organization—because my kid wanted to play and I understood that I could play a support role to help the program continue. And we had a coach who was definitely not afraid to ask.

Our ministry team determined that we could ask parents to serve once every six (1:6) weeks on a rotation—designed to fit even the busiest schedules. The method we use is a phone call from volunteers to parents whose kids have a regular attendance pattern. Of course, some of these phone calls are more successful than others. I've tried a variety of methods—in fact, here are three possibilities. Pick the one you believe is the best approach (hint—only one will work!).

The Bribery Method

Hello, Mr. Johnson, I work with your son Daniel in the five-year-old room. This weekend he happened to mention your love for great coffee. What if I were to say that there would be a grande café latte—extra foam with a touch of nutmeg—just sitting in the five-year-old room with your name on it every six weeks, and all you have to do is show up and help me. What do you say? Okay then, what if I throw in a box of donuts?

The Guilt Method

Well, Mr. Johnson, I hate to bring this up but they are your kids. If you didn't want to be a parent, maybe you should have thought about that before bringing two new lives into this world. But since you did, there's something that comes with it called 'responsibility'. . . .

The Vision Method

Mr. Johnson, I notice that you've been attending our church regularly and I wanted to find out how we're serving your family. Great. I also called to let you know that we like to give every parent the opportunity to come in and experience Promiseland with their child—as an adult helper. An adult helper is a volunteer who serves once every six weeks. It's a chance for you to peek into your child's world and serve at the same time.

The 1:6 program honors parents by giving them an opportunity to step into Promiseland and participate in this amazing hour that their child experiences every Sunday. During the phone call, we make it clear that this is an invitation to do more than just watch: "We need you to be an extra set of hands to help serve kids. You don't lead anything. You don't have to plan anything. There's no preparation. You just show up once in a six-week period."

The majority of the people contacted say yes. Once every six weeks is an easy time block to fit in, and is a fairly light commitment. The program does, though, require serious ministry planning. And that preparation begins with a one-minute vision cast developed to be shared over the phone. But the payoff for all this effort is a flow of new volunteers who come into the ministry, with the potential that their commitment might deepen. To borrow another baseball analogy—we now have runners on base.

Every-Week Volunteers

What is so significant to people that they would volunteer every week in children's ministry? Simple—it's kids, and not just their own. These people don't want to work in just any ministry, because they have a specific passion to reach children. They look at their calendars and rearrange weekends because making a difference in kids' lives is a priority based on how God wired them up.

Dan is one of those people. But he didn't just show up on his own in Promiseland, he had help getting there. A ministry leader watched Dan begin as a special event volunteer, then return as a 1:6 adult helper. During a conversation this leader said, "I can see some potential in you, Dan. Are you enjoying this?" He went on to challenge Dan to consider a weekly role leading a small group. An important factor in the story is that this recruiting occurred as part of an existing relationship. It wasn't a cold hit in the middle of a hallway or in a phone call from someone Dan didn't know.

Our senior pastor, Bill Hybels, says that personal relationships are a key to success in volunteer recruiting—just as in evangelism. "You have a much higher likelihood of successfully inviting someone into service if they know you and trust you," he explains.

> You have a much higher likelihood of successfully inviting someone into service if they know you and trust you.
>
> *Bill Hybels*

Bill goes on to suggest meeting over a cup of coffee and sharing a well-thought-out, personal ministry vision and invitation. He offers this example:

"Fred, the sixty minutes I spend with kids in Promiseland each Sunday is the best sixty minutes of my week. I might get to teach a kid from a non-churched family how to pray. I might tell a kid from a broken home that God loves him. Or maybe I can take a kid who's scared and put my arms around him and tell him he doesn't need to be afraid because God is his friend. Fred, would you be willing to come one time—with me—to see what God is doing in Promiseland?"[1]

Some people serve every week from the outset; others graduate to this frequency from special event or 1:6 status. Whatever the path, it's a significant time investment. To gain insight on a volunteer's journey toward committing to every-week service, I talked to Dan about his experience. He said, "It was a big deal for me to say yes to being an every-week volunteer. On one side, I was weighing what my family life was like on the weekends. We had a boat, and that created good family time. My kids were involved in soccer leagues and played all the time. And I'm a salesperson who needs to make some sales calls during the weekend."

But the leader who talked with him wisely said, "Dan, only you can grapple with all those issues. I'm asking you to pray and see what God tells you to do."

Dan said, "When I would pray, this opportunity started to seem irresistible. I wanted to make a difference in the lives of ten kids as a small group leader. I just couldn't walk away from it. So I said yes. Fact is, our whole family started serving in Promiseland. It was amazing to us that we didn't care so much about going boating on the weekends anymore. And the kids didn't want to sign up for as many soccer leagues, so our schedule got a little easier. What it did inside of our family was more than worth the effort it took to reschedule our calendar."

Dan's story is typical of people who decide that they want to become part of a wild vision. Just remember that every-week volunteers—whether they lead a small group, play for the band, serve in administrative roles, or are part of a student helper team—need consistent reminders that their service is significant. So tell them often that what they do really matters and that kids will be in heaven one day because of them. And make sure their puzzle piece fits in the ministry, and that it continues to fit over time. Coaches watch their people to make sure the fit stays right. People at this level of commitment need and deserve personal recruiting and care.

Core Volunteers

Over time, something big happens to the most committed every-week volunteers. They take one more step in their commitment by becoming a core volunteer—a coach responsible for other leaders, a room leader, or possibly a ministry leadership team member. These people say, "No longer am I a participant in the vision, I *own* this vision. You can count on me. I'm here for the long haul." And so they become a stakeholder of the wild vision.

Everyone
Special Event Volunteers
1:6 Adult Volunteers
Every Week Volunteers, Students

Coaches & Core
Vision to own the mission of ministry

How does it happen from a volunteer's perspective? I asked our friend Dan. He said, "I knew that when I was a small group leader, I was making a difference in ten kid's lives and that was awesome. But then a key leader challenged me to become a coach." (A coach in Promiseland leads and shepherds other adult leaders, and is the highest level of volunteer commitment.)

"When I signed up as a coach," he said, "I understood that I was now going to multiply my ministry impact. I was going to build into ten leaders who were each going to build into ten kids." When the right vision is shared with the right volunteer, and he or she fully understands the significance of a key role, a ministry gets stronger. This vision casting and invitation to join a ministry's committed core has credibility when a senior leader delivers it.

The layered circles image illustrates a key goal in sharing the dream in different ways—to move people through different depths of commitment. Obviously, this path must follow God's lead and guidance. And along the way, kids benefit from a strong ministry, because everyone serves in a layer of the vision that fits them just right.

Let's look at baseball one last time. Another lesson I learned is that it's a team sport—and that "team" includes parents. We sold candy bars together, brought juice boxes together, and worked the concession stand together. Sharing your ministry dream with the rest of your church is also a team sport.

> Kids benefit from a strong ministry, because everyone serves in a layer of the vision that fits them just right.

At times, the director needs to cast the vision. Other times, several players in your ministry will broadcast the vision—and hopefully hit a home run. But for a children's ministry to succeed over time, a constant stream of new folks must catch the vision. That means several people from your ministry must join the recruiting game—and be on constant lookout for opportunities to have strategic cups of coffee.

Without doubt, recruiting is a long game and involves a lot of work. And that's no surprise to God. Fortunately, Jesus' words in Matthew 9:37–38 share the secret of how to play with an expectation to win: "The harvest is plentiful but the workers are few. Ask the Lord of the harvest, therefore, to send out workers into his harvest field."

Chapter 7

LESSONS LEARNED

How to Treat Volunteers

One of my favorite books is *Children's Letters to God* by Stuart Hample and Eric Marshall. One letter is a request from Ginny, who asks God to create a new holiday to fill the void between Christmas and Easter. Her reason is simple: "There is nothing good in there now."[1] Anyone who lives in Chicago from January to April wholeheartedly shares that sentiment. It's generally cold, windy, and gray—and that's on the nice days.

To add some heat to this meteorologically challenged stretch on the calendar, Promiseland lavishes special thanks on our volunteers one weekend each February or March. The kids throw parties for their small group leaders, we bring in food for each service, and we even ask parents to join the festivities. One year we alerted the whole church about the event through an article in the weekend printed program, describing reasons why children appreciate volunteers:

Promiseland Celebrates Volunteer Appreciation This Weekend.
So what do kids have to say about Promiseland volunteers?

"Miss Jamie lets me say stuff without interrupting me. I wish my brother was like that."
(Thanks to all the small group leaders who really listen to and love our kids.)

"I like the someone that puts all the Goldfishies [crackers] in the cups . . . they must be a good counter."
(Thanks to all the volunteers who arrive hours early or stay late to set up Promiseland and make it a place kids love.)

"I like the band, especially the guy playing the electric drums—it's way cool."
(Thanks to all the musicians, vocalists, and teachers who creatively and relevantly teach the Bible to our kids.)

"The lady at the name tag table always remembers me, but I kind of forget her name."
(Thanks to all the administrative volunteers who make Promiseland safe and fun.)

"Sure are lots of big people in Promiseland today!"
(Thank you to all adult volunteers and student helpers, including those who come in on weekdays—you make Promiseland the best hour of every kid's week . . . it can't happen without you!)

Now it's your turn. Please say thank you to the volunteers in Promiseland as you pick up your child after this service. They are easy to find—look for the taller people.

Know Why

Sometimes it can be so refreshing to hear a child's perspective! Can you imagine how honored the people felt who put the "Goldfishies" in cups each week? And they thought no one noticed!

As director of Promiseland, it is important for me to know how our volunteers feel about serving. Many show up faithfully year after year, which is a good sign. But the ever-learning leader in me wonders why they do that. So I hosted an open house for a group of veteran volunteers with ten or more years of experience, and asked them to answer one question: "Why do you serve in Promiseland?" Here are some of their responses:

- The love I have for other leaders that I serve with in the room.
- I get my weekly "fix" of love.
- Knowing parents give us their most important thing in life.
- It's definitely the best hour of my week!
- Promiseland is where you are more important than task.
- It's great to see life-change in little people.
- Because we're actually being served by the people in Promiseland.

Collecting reasons why people volunteer was easy with this dedicated group—I just asked them. And I love the personal nature of each reason. Learning why volunteers leave Promiseland, on the other hand, is not nearly as

> If we recruit well, then we must be just as deliberate with how we care for people once they're on board.

easy. But this knowledge can be equally valuable—and maybe even more important when it reflects the realities and qualities of ministry life we invite people into. If we recruit well (with a vision that fits just right, of course) then we must be just as deliberate with how we care for people once they're on board. When this doesn't happen, the results are predictable—volunteers quit.

Four Lessons on How to Treat Volunteers

Across years of making almost every mistake possible, I have consolidated my learning into four key lessons about how to treat people who join our ministry. These lessons came from years of work with volunteers that taught me there are four big problems sure to prevent successful serving. I tend to think of these four problem areas as "ministry monsters" that can slip into our ministries unnoticed. Each has a unique strategy for taking

people down. And each will wreak havoc on the ministry until leaders listen carefully to the personal needs of volunteers and respond appropriately. You may have seen or felt the pain of their handiwork, and now it's time to deal with them out in the open. For the rest of this chapter, the monsters will speak for themselves—with each followed by a plan to rid our ministries of them.

Used and Abused

Hello, I'm used and abused. Yes, that's my name—Used and Abused. And nobody understands volunteers like I do. I see them for who they really are—real people with real needs. But what about the leaders of this ministry? To them, volunteers are just worker ants pushing dirt from one pile to the other. And the only reason leaders are glad to see volunteers on Sunday is because people have shown up to do something for them.

Leaders say, "Good morning. I'm so glad to see you this morning." That can be translated to: "Good morning. I'm so glad I'm using you to get my job done. The donuts are right over there in case your power cells run low. Now get back to work, drone!" Volunteers get used and abused, just like me. Let's stick together so we can figure out that we don't have to put up with it. Remember, nobody understands volunteers like I do.

Lesson 1: "Value Me"

Volunteers are smart people—and not just because they select children's ministry as the place to use their gifts and talents! They know the difference between a ministry that really appreciates them and one that is simply relieved that the workload can now be shared. To keep that insidious character called Used and Abused out of a ministry, leaders at all levels must realize that every volunteer wants to say, "Value me. Please don't make me feel like you ask me to come on Sunday morning just so that you can use me to get your ministry done."

One clear sign that the "Value Me" lesson needs serious attention is when volunteers refer to the ministry with the word "your." When people feel that their work is unimportant, they will distance themselves from owning any part of the ministry—and the pronouns "we, our, and us" will be conspicuously absent. This is an indication of a fixable problem, so let's turn toward a solution.

Jesus often reminded people of their high value. For example, we see this in his parables in Luke 15 about the lost sheep, lost coin, and lost prodigal son. In the story of Mary and Martha, he makes the point that people are more important than the work they get done. Jesus also lived out a model of valuing volunteers with his own team— consider how much time he spent alone

> Jesus often reminded people of their high value.

with them instead of with a crowd. Those disciples must have felt honored to have Jesus so generously give them the precious commodity of his time.

Leaders can help people feel valued in many ways. Give praise freely and often. Make it normal for your ministry to thank and appreciate every volunteer who shows up on Sunday morning. I love it on weekends when I hear leaders say simple words like, "We appreciate you making this a priority in your life," "We couldn't do it without you," or "Thanks, you're making kingdom impact today!"

Some volunteers respond even more to the right questions. Pat is a long-time volunteer in our toddler room. She describes what makes her feel valued: "Our coaches are fantastic about coming around during the course of the time that we're serving and checking in with us, wanting to know what's going on in our lives, making sure that everything is running smoothly in the room, and asking if we need any more help or supplies," she says. "Just that effort makes us feel like we're the most important people in the world."

To honor all your volunteers and staff, consider a ministry year kick-off party or end-of-year celebration. Or plan a volunteer appreciation weekend midway through the year. Promiseland invests significant time and creativity into these events, and the payoff is worth it when Used and Abused is nowhere to be found.

In her book *Leadership Skills,* Emily Morrison lists the top nine reasons people stop volunteering.[2] Not surprising is that four of the nine relate to feeling undervalued. I invite Used and Abused into the ministry when I don't carefully listen to where new people want to serve, and when I stop listening to them after they begin to serve. If volunteers are to live out 1 Corinthians 15:58—"Stand firm. Let nothing move you. Always give yourselves fully to the work of the Lord, because you know that your labor in the Lord is not in vain"—then I must tell them and show them that they and all they do are valued.

Isolation

Hi, my name is Isolation. There's nothing bad about me, I'm just addicted to loneliness. Not mine—your volunteers'. I feed on it. At first it was just a light snack once in a while, but soon the hunger grew. And now I am not satisfied until as many people as possible are completely isolated. How can I hurt a ministry by making volunteers feel alone? Good question.

Many of my colleagues go for the more obvious weaknesses: dishonesty, sexual impropriety;

you know, the biggies. That's the difference between them and me. They want volunteers to get kicked out of ministry. I want them to quit. It is true that isolation is much subtler, but here is my theory: no matter what anybody says, nobody likes to feel totally alone. I know I don't. Being alone in ministry work just becomes no fun. And once a volunteer has reached that stage, quitting is the next logical conclusion. Don't sell isolation short. It may be a lost art, but it's making a comeback.

Lesson 2: "Connect Me"

Volunteers want to be known and to know the other people they work alongside. Relationships are key to creating a spirit of unity that makes serving feel more like contributing to a family project than dutifully checking off chores.

Once again consider how Jesus modeled the value of connecting with his disciples. He walked along the road with them and engaged them in conversation. They ate together. They went boating together. They did ministry together. Jesus did not allow Isolation to take any ground inside his team. John 17:6–19 records Jesus' final prayer for his group, in which he longs for their unity. And why? He says in verse 13, "I say these things while I am still in the world, so that they may have the full measure of my joy within them."

Togetherness helps deliver God's full measure of joy because no volunteer wants to be anonymous. They want leaders to know them, and they want to know and be known by others. What's not to like about being part of a great team where you walk into a room and everybody greets you by name and says, "Hey, how you doing? Glad you're here!" Joy, laughter, and a community where

> Togetherness helps deliver God's full measure of joy because no volunteer wants to be anonymous.

people know each other—shouldn't we want all of that in our ministries?

But responding to "Connect Me" doesn't just happen on its own—ministry organization plays a big role in enabling connection. Small groups designed for adult small group leaders are a great start to ensure that these dedicated volunteers have a place to belong and receive the same kind of shepherd's care that they constantly provide for children. Serving teams for administrators, creative communicators, musicians, and others will achieve a similar result—people serving *together* instead of simply near each other.

Linda, another committed Promiseland team member, has "serving teams" that come in on specific days each week to perform administrative tasks and assemble the lesson materials into plastic tubs and bins for the weekend. Every one of her teams identifies themselves by their day of the week (i.e., the Tuesday Team), has committed members, and regularly enjoys God's full measure of joy because they serve together. Volunteers in the children's ministry at Antioch EV Free Church in Antioch, Illinois, formed their own version of weekday serving teams, and called them the Bin Babes!

Of course it takes more than a catchy name to "Connect Me." Specific and consistent time must be allotted to non-task-related discussions. The VIP treatment for small group leader huddles (described in chapter 5) always includes time for people to share personal issues and prayer requests. Although their time is limited, huddle members meet forty-two consecutive weeks, which allows conversation to go deeper over time. And when something major happens in a member's life, a team rich with relational equity is there to support him or her. I constantly hear people describe the team they serve with as their family.

Ministry relationships stand in strong contrast to the reality that in much of the marketplace people feel alone. People there often don't want to share what's really going on inside of them. Impression management is common, and Isolation routinely wins.

But it shouldn't be allowed a ministry victory. A paradigm shift is often necessary to establish small groups for leaders or serving teams for every position—and it requires time to accomplish. I admit it took awhile, but finally I tuned in to our volunteers who were saying, "Connect Me," and we made those big changes. Now, Isolation is headed back to being a lost art.

Power Monger

Hey, you—I am the humongous Power Monger! It's my job to make volunteers feel like they never get any power. I love it when they say, "Everyone decides everything without me! They never ask my opinion!" My first mission is always to make leaders think that volunteers are feeble, flabby, and just too puny to be of any good. Who cares if volunteers want to help make decisions about the ministry but leaders don't give them a chance? Even passive aggression is fine with me—"forgetting" to tell volunteers about changes until it's too late to give input, for instance, or not telling them there's a new book full of vision for a better children's ministry because they might dare to ask if they can talk about a new idea. [Okay, I wedged in that last one!]

So volunteers have all decisions made for them because I make sure the big, strong children's ministry leaders decide everything! I also make sure that volunteers are never told why changes get made.

Lesson 3: "Include Me"

The Power Monger is a unique character because he does his dirty work on the staff and leadership of a ministry, rather than personally affecting volunteers. I don't believe any person takes a position in children's ministry with the intent to be powerful, but the temptation is always there. Everyone hired into a ministry role has a responsibility to deliver results, and thus is tempted to open the door when Power Monger knocks. Thoughts about how to include volunteers are easy to set aside.

The most important line of difference that should exist between a volunteer and a paid staff position is the word "paid." All too often, the word "power" tends to sneak in as part of a perceived benefits package, a chasm forms, and weird decisions get made. A ministry develops strategy without asking for input from volunteers with marketplace experience in this very area. Or volunteers don't receive updates on ministry direction or progress because we, as staff, assume that volunteers' lives are so busy that they don't want involvement with leadership issues. We don't slow down the speeding ministry train to ask for input because we believe there's no time for volunteers.

I wish I could tell you I have never thought or done any of that, but I have. Too many times I have heard that my lack of communication or failure to include volunteers in planning disappointed and hurt the volunteers that I love to serve beside. A Great Kid-Venture isn't a solo journey—and we can learn a better way from biblical "Include Me" examples.

Consider how inclusive Jesus was with his disciples. Scripture records several occasions when he spent time carefully explaining the meaning of his parables and other teachings. Jesus also deliberately prepared them for his departure. John 16:16–33 describes how Jesus carefully explained his upcoming death and resurrection—Jesus wanted his ministry team to know what to expect from him, and what to expect from their role.

For instance, when Peter felt like a failure, Jesus in essence said, "Peter, get back into the game. You are still part of the mission, so feed my sheep!" Later, the book of Acts describes Peter's emergence as a major figure in building the early Church—he surely felt included. Jesus also developed a new opportunity to be part of the ministry when he sent his followers out in pairs to do ministry on their own—they

> **Jesus made sure his volunteers felt they were right in the middle of the action.**

surely felt included. The trend I see is that Jesus made sure his volunteers felt they were right in the middle of the action.

Volunteers can and should be in the same position in children's ministry today. If you're a leader, then make inclusion a deliberate part of your style. Do you invite volunteers onto the highest reaches of leadership? Have you established a reliable communication channel to keep everyone in your ministry informed? Is asking volunteers for input a regular practice?

Nancy, a veteran Promiseland volunteer, explains the impact of leaders asking volunteers questions: "One of the things that really helps me feel included is when our room leader comes around and checks on how we are doing. But what I appreciate even more is that Sue and Pat [Cimo] occasionally stop by my room and say, 'Nancy, how is it going?' And I know they really want to know what's working and what's not working. They ask for my ideas and my opinions. And I've noticed many of those ideas are implemented. They really listen and really care about what we see on the front line."

Recently I discovered what I believe to be the high-water mark for an inclusive structure. The American Red Cross is the largest volunteer organization in the country, with more than 1.2 million unpaid workers who make up 97 percent of the organization's total workforce. I assumed that the other 3 percent—the paid staff—must handle all the leadership and management. Wrong. From their top executive at headquarters to the staff of each local branch, every paid leadership position has a volunteer counterpart with whom they share responsibility.[3] This example proves that "Include Me" can be taken to extraordinary levels.

In most children's ministries, staff members are few and far between. If this is your situation, the questions to wrestle with still focus on inclusion. Do the same one or two people decide everything? Are communication channels open between leadership and the rest of the team? Do people use those channels frequently?

What if you are a volunteer reading this, and right now you know that your "Include Me" desire is ignored? Two suggestions. First, don't dismiss the concern or act like you didn't read this chapter. Second, schedule some time outside of your ministry setting to talk over your feelings with the leader of your ministry. Focus the conversation toward the increased involvement you are prepared to offer, and the value your service can bring to the ministry. Statements such as "I would love to help out with _____" are more productive than "You should _____." I have a hunch your ministry leader will welcome your help and fresh ideas. And when that happens, any Power Monger monster slithering around the ministry will become a bit weaker.

Stagnation

Are your volunteers feeling bored? Lackluster, perhaps? Has serving in your ministry lost its shine? Do volunteers show up on weekends unprepared and just "wing it"? Do people think, "If I didn't have to volunteer I could sleep in today"?

Well, if one or more of these symptoms describes any of your volunteers, then I'm glad! They, and hundreds like them, are in my hands now—the grip of Stagnation! My presence is characterized by feelings of boredom, lack of purpose, and a growing dislike for children and churches. Yes, I said children. You'd be surprised how I, Stagnation, can change a heart. Eventually, this prompts a volunteer to quit and maybe even to give ministry leaders a piece of his or her mind. That causes excitement for a moment or two, and then it's back to the normal, dull-time music!

You may ask, "Stagnation, why do you want to torment us?" I think that's a funny question because I've been doing my thing for quite a while. Haven't you noticed the bored looks on kids' faces every Sunday morning? I've already taken care of lots of them. So it's nothing personal—volunteers are just next in line.

Lesson 4: "Challenge Me"

To prevent Stagnation from parking in ministry, volunteers must be challenged. This should be no surprise because very few people want to do the very same thing for a long time. And "long time" is different for every individual. Volunteers must be surprised every now and then, feel like they are growing, and believe that ministry demands their best.

Think of how Jesus did all that with his disciples. First, he took ordinary guys—fisherman, tax collectors, etc.—and changed their careers and called them to a bigger life mission. For three years he helped them grow in a variety of ways. They watched Jesus perform miraculous healings, participated in extraordinary events such as feeding thousands from one sack lunch, and received radical love that knew no end. Then they were challenged to reach the world. You don't read any verses in the Bible that say the disciples were bored or disinterested in ministry. Jesus knew exactly when to change someone's name, how to ask someone to leave everything behind to follow him, and what words to speak to build a person up. And after he went up to heaven, Jesus' followers gave him their best.

Jesus saw the potential inside people. Isn't that exactly how ministry needs to view others? All people are potential Christ-followers, a truth at the heartbeat of evangelism. In much the same way, those who step up to work in children's ministry have the potential to

> Jesus saw the potential inside people.

make a kingdom difference. If you view people through that lens, then ministry looks full of possibilities.

I know one of the most important reasons that volunteers aren't continually challenged in ministry is because leaders are just thankful that people show up. To challenge someone might drive him or her away—it might be perceived as a bait-and-switch. The truth is, though, that when someone joins a ministry for the right reasons—because of a vision that fits just right—he or she knowingly takes a step out of the stands and onto the playing field. So make it an exciting game!

Challenge people who are gifted leaders to grow their leadership through taking on more responsibility. Challenge gifted communicators to expand their role in large group time. Challenge an administrator to develop new processes to make the ministry run smoother. And if you're reading this and feel underchallenged in whatever role you have, take the initiative to request more. Asking for people to give their best and take their involvement to a new level is done in every corner of the marketplace, so it's not a new idea to shy away from.

We have a seventeen-year volunteer in Promiseland named Dave. Every few years, leaders challenge Dave to consider a different role. Sometimes it's a step up on the leadership ladder; sometimes it's a lateral step to a different position. He started as a small group leader, moved on to a variety of coach positions, has served as a coordinator overseeing the second- through fifth-grade area, and is now a leader on the team that organizes our conferences and mentors other children's ministry leaders, both domestically and inter-nationally. The loss to our ministry would have been great if someone along the way had thought, "He has built such a great team as a coach, and I can't lose him. I need to just keep him where he is."

Dave is an entrepreneurial businessman. He's the kind of guy who loves a new challenge. Had Dave felt underutilized or bored at any time, he might have walked. People just like Dave are in every children's ministry, looking to be challenged. I know we haven't always done well in this area, and that Promiseland has let some people feel unchallenged to the point that they decided to leave. I can't judge the ministry impact of Stagnation's grip on these people, but I can work to prevent its icy fingers from return-ing. You can, too.

When People Abound the Pulse Pounds!

Too much time went by before I fully understood that I must value, con-nect, include, and challenge volunteers. And when that happens, they soar—and so does Promiseland. In an area of the church where the num-ber of paid staff is a tiny fraction of the workforce, the health of volunteerism determines the strength of the ministry's heartbeat. And when people abound the pulse pounds!

So four ministry monsters taught me four big lessons that I'm glad I eventually learned—although at the time none of this was too much fun. Have these four slipped into your ministry? Or are there different ones you must deal with?

No one but you can fully answer these questions, so make it a passion for your ministry to learn why people stay and why people leave. Organize an informal volunteer meeting to gather comments. Ask three people this weekend. Maybe you can start with whoever puts the Goldfishies in cups. You will honor people just by asking them why they serve. The results promise to be eye-opening. And it will be a great warm-up exercise for the next chapter.

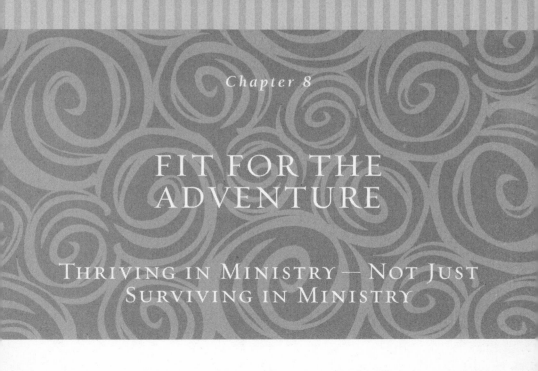

Chapter 8

FIT FOR THE ADVENTURE

THRIVING IN MINISTRY — NOT JUST SURVIVING IN MINISTRY

You have brains in your head.
You have feet in your shoes.
You can steer yourself
any direction you choose.
You're on your own. And you know what you know.
And YOU are the guy who'll decide where to go . . .

Oh, the Places You'll Go! by Dr. Seuss[1]

In real life, sometimes you must steer toward a place that you'd rather avoid. I went to one of those places recently—the hospital for partial knee replacement surgery. It amazes me that this procedure is even possible. In a world where nobody has figured out how to make the plastic bags in cereal boxes easy to open and close, doctors can go into my leg to replace worn parts and then reseal it.

I required surgery because years of deterioration had weakened my right knee. According to my doctor, I had used up the knee's cartilage. "How can that be?" I wondered. Is cartilage really a consumable body part? And what was my left knee doing while my right knee wore out? Only one logical answer came to mind—years of twisting, bending, and turning to the motions of Promiseland songs had taken their toll. The apparent laziness of my left knee during all that dancing remains a mystery.

I felt relief after this dreaded surgery, but only for a moment. No one had explained that an even more daunting challenge comes from two words rarely mentioned before the procedure: *physical therapy*. When I fully regained my senses a couple days after surgery, I discovered that my brand-new knee was nowhere close to being ready to use. So I learned a lot about physical therapy the hard way—while in the midst of it, which I still am while writing this book. And during those long, painful weeks, I realized that strong parallels exist between the regimen of rehabilitation and ministry life.

What I Learned from Physical Therapy

One clear similarity is that therapy is hard—and so is ministry. For some people, that probably was a comforting statement to read, because ministry success attracts far more attention than its struggles. The truth is, when ministry is a challenge, that isn't an indication of failure or ineptitude. It's simply a reality. There will be tough times of conflict, disappointment, and loss, so ministry requires a heart and soul that are alive and full to the point of resiliency. This requirement applies to workers and leaders on all levels. Knowing that challenges are normal and to be expected helps me remember that I am not crazy or incompetent. Jesus said in John 16:33, "In this world you will have trouble. But take heart! I have overcome the world."

Let's continue the parallels. Physical therapy is an activity I must choose to go through for my knee to once again be fit enough to walk, jog, and dance to Promiseland music. Staying fit for a run in any capacity within children's ministry requires a similar choice: you can learn how to do ministry life well, or you can hobble along and have a tougher time down the road.

I'll say this as clearly as I can by setting aside the medical analogy for a moment: it is very possible to build or work in an incredible children's ministry and lose your heart and soul for God along the way. That applies to leaders, paid staff, and volunteers. I don't want that to happen to you or me. More importantly, God doesn't want anyone to develop a hard heart or shriveled soul as a consequence of building his kingdom. But if you're not careful, that can happen. So let's explore how to be careful.

> It is very possible to build or work in an incredible children's ministry and lose your heart and soul for God along the way.

Therapy requires a personal commitment to work that no one can do for me. In other words, I must practice *self-leadership* to succeed. The hardest person for me to lead is me. Self-leadership must be my top priority—as many leaders who have gone before us have clearly shown. Lack it and the results are predictable.

This point is proved by an observation by John Maxwell in *The Maxwell Leadership Bible,* "More than two-thirds of all biblical leaders finish poorly."[2] The specific reasons why most failed vary, but all are related to some type of self-leadership lapse. Consider Noah, "a righteous man, blameless in his generation" (Gen. 6:9 ESV). He led a great life until the end, when he began to overdrink, which resulted in cursing his grandson. Or King David, described as a man after God's own heart (Acts 13:22). Despite leading a nation, his personal failures resulted in adultery and an incredible sequence of sins that hurt many along the way. Neither Noah nor David made a conscious decision to abruptly abandon their sense of right and wrong—both just relaxed their self-leadership over time.

Unfortunately, no one could be my substitute through the pain and strain of physical therapy, just as no one can develop and practice self-leadership for me. My years in ministry help me see this issue clearly: the greatest gift I can bring to my ministry—kids, volunteers, and paid staff—is a heart that is full and surrendered to God. For me to live with God exclusively in the center takes constant attention that is punctuated with hard decisions. Proverbs 4:23 says, "Above all else, guard your heart, for it is the wellspring of life." Self-leadership involves the options each of us face and forms the backdrop to important lessons we must learn about choices that involve perspective, pace, and load.

Perspective

Physical therapy focuses on overcoming physical challenges. At times it requires strength training, sometimes it calls for aerobic conditioning, and other times it calls for agility exercises. The initial hurdle I faced was knee flexibility. When I first arrived at the therapist's office, my knee could only bend 55 degrees. The goal was 110. My daily routine involved leg lifts until I reached fatigue, stretching past the point of pain, and an all-out battle to make that knee flex a little farther. I longed for the day when the therapist would announce that my progress reached 90 degrees, which would enable me to once again ride in a car and climb stairs. (Although with dirty clothes piling up in the basement laundry area, the car ride was definitely more appealing.)

I spent hours on the floor painfully stretching and faithfully exercising. While doing so, my mind often drifted to a song used often in Promiseland called *Bend My Knee,* and specifically to the chorus:

> *I'm not gonna bend my knee*
> *To anybody but you*
> *I'm not gonna bend my knee*
> *Oh, oh, no*
> *I'm not gonna bend my knee*
> *I answer only to you*
> *I'm not gonna bend my knee*
> *To anybody but you*[3]

As I hummed this song, I found myself wishing that my character were as difficult to bend as my knee. Specifically I wondered, *Do I give all my worship—bend my knee—to God alone?* The honest answer was no, which pushed me to dig deeper and look at my life from a new perspective. I realized that to guard my heart, I must choose to worship only God.

So I admitted what motivates me— an exercise that revealed my worship goes in many directions other than God.

> I must choose to worship only God.

Sometimes I bow down to the approval of others, which gives them too much power in my life. Other times I kneel at the altar of image management—intentionally projecting the impression that all is well, even when that's not entirely true. Both of these idols stem from a fear of what people think about me—which can grip me so tight that sinful words, ideas, or actions spray out. I also saw that material things can capture my heart's desire.

This flow of honest evaluation continued. I thought of the times that I wrap too much of my identity around my position as Promiseland director. *Any* leader, paid staff, or volunteer can easily let his or her ego inflate because of title, status, or ministry tenure. A big problem exists when healthy servant leadership yields to a desire to be served. This ego problem is often conveniently dismissed as delegation, optimizing efficiency, or some other clever-sounding justification. Don't read this wrong—it's good to delegate and look for better ways to distribute work. That's a leader's job. The sinful twist occurs when it's done to benefit the person in charge instead of the ministry—or when the leader's agenda starts to matter more than others' agendas. After all, everyone should expect that the highest-ranking person is the one who knows what's best for the ministry. Yes, I've gone there and done all that. Yuck! Whenever my title makes me feel that I'm better than other people, I've lost perspective.

Ill-placed knee bending is not a small issue to God. Jesus describes the *greatest* commandment in Mark 12:30, "You shall love the Lord your God with all your heart, and with all your soul, and with all your mind, and with all your strength." This means don't worship anything else—a directive also described in the first two commandments of the big ten. Fortunately, God wants to help us keep him at the center of our lives, so I now spend long stretches of time talking about this with him and asking what needs attention. I find that confessing to God that something or someone else receives my worship helps me gain healthy perspective and places him back as the exclusive center of my life. His response is always love and forgiveness and fresh focus on how he sees me. The only approval, image, or identity I need to worry about is in God's eyes. I must choose to worship only him.

Pace

Once my knee started to bend, the next leg of therapy kicked in—aerobic conditioning. Increased circulation helps eliminate swelling, so I hobbled onto an elliptical training machine. If you're unfamiliar with this apparatus, the concept is pretty easy to understand. Your feet go onto ski-like boards that are connected to a flywheel with poles that you grab and pump with your arms—creating a mixture of cross-country skiing and jogging. The benefit from this piece of equipment is exhilarating exercise with very little impact on the knees. It sure gets the ole heart pumping!

When you hop on the elliptical trainer (you can hop; I'm lifted on), the small screen asks for the total time you want to work out and your age. The machine then sets a reasonable exercise program that includes an appropriate target heart rate. When the screen reads "Begin Exercise," I'm off to the races. Okay, maybe not right away. I start slowly, pumping my arms and doing the best I can with my partially replaced leg. But every time I reach the recommended speed and get into a smooth rhythm, something strange happens. For some reason, I become bold and start pushing a little harder and going a little faster. Then a little faster. And faster still. Eventually I go too fast for my own good, and the machine flashes this message:

Decrease speed to maintain targeted heart rate.

These profound words from a machine resonate deep within my soul. I know that at times I work in ministry at a pace that's not good—sometimes at an almost dangerous pace. No machine warns me that it's happening, but nevertheless, there are some very clear signs. For instance, at home or work I may fall into a pattern of frequently saying, "I don't have enough time for that." This usually means I've overscheduled my calendar and don't want interruptions to those plans. This is tragic because it robs me of the chance to fully experience life. As C. S. Lewis said, "The truth is, of course, that what one calls the interruptions are precisely one's real life—the life God is sending one day by day."[4]

Another sign of working at a too-fast pace is increasing cynicism. Or I might stop attending church services because I feel too exhausted to go. Maybe it's when I start realizing I am not as loving as I used to be toward other people, or that joy in life is wearing thin—possibly completely gone. The common denominator in all these situations is a lack of meaningful moments for God to refresh and refuel me, since those are real easy to skip (limp) over because no one notices. Well, no one except God and me. I know that I must choose to slow down and spend time with God, but sometimes I don't.

Whatever the indicator, the cause is quite consistent—I overschedule and that leads me to overreact. Then comes the belief that I must go to work early and stay late. This eventually morphs into working constantly, which is not a sustainable pace. Granted, there are exceptions to this, such as the extra hours necessary before a big event. The obvious problem emerges when this accelerated pace becomes a routine rather than an exception. And even though my arms, legs, and mind can help me reach high speed, my heart is generally the first to feel the impact. Once again, I know I must choose to slow down and spend time with God, but for some reason I don't.

> I must choose to slow down and spend time with God.

When my pace is too fast, discouragement trails close behind about how I'm doing as a wife, mother, and friend. At high speeds, my leadership effectiveness diminishes. It's amazing that people who serve in ministry can work too hard and spiritually starve themselves. This doesn't only apply to leaders—I've seen plenty of volunteers ignore their family, friends, and careers so they can spend more time working at church. And in the absence of self-leadership, they might even be applauded for their commitment. Until, of course, the pace burns them out and they leave. We need a solution for this problem. And fortunately, it is not too complicated.

When soaked with perspiration from running too fast, I remember Psalm 23 and how Jesus wants to lead me beside quiet waters to restore my soul. In other words, he wants to spend time in a quiet place with me. This means I must intentionally slow down—sometimes way down. If that calls for canceling commitments, then I do it. Every day I need to make time to be with God in meaningful ways, because I must relate to God before I can serve him. It could be a few minutes listening to worship music. Possibly a two-hour walk through nature. Or even just a couple hours of recreational fun. I know that I must regularly schedule early mornings to read the Bible and write in a journal—two key disciplines that keep me connected to God. Any effort to change the pace of life should start with reestablishing a healthy rhythm of time with God designed to keep my heart fully alive.

No one else renews my heart and soul like God. No one else speaks as much deep truth about my character as God. And nothing else has as great an impact on the rest of my day as moments shared with God. When ministry is hard, God's power strengthens me from the inside out.

And time with God brings clarity on what is a priority versus simply busyness. This is what I've learned: My personal relationship with God is a high priority. My family is a high priority. My friendships are high priorities. My health is a high priority. I must start the rest of my priority list after these. This prioritization helps develop the confidence to say no to activities so life can become sane. In the likely case that you don't have anyone in ministry telling you your pace is too fast, I'm going to flash this important message to you:

Slow down and spend time with God.

Load

The next big physical challenge waiting for me was strength training. My therapist instructed me to use one-and-one-half-pound ankle weights during leg lifts. Back at home, I reasoned that I could get much stronger if I used four pound weights instead. This would surely impress my therapist and possibly accelerate therapy! Wrong.

Instead of a quick route to gaining strength, my overambitious effort resulted in immediate swelling and increased pain. I tried to do too much in therapy, and I tend to do the very same thing in ministry.

One year Promiseland decided to put together a Christmas musical as an evangelistic tool to reach families. We planned one Sunday afternoon show. But when that performance sold out so quickly that many parents didn't get tickets, we added two more shows. Regrettably, we scheduled all three on the same weekend, in addition to our regular ministry program.

This musical, initially designed to include a cast of 30 kids, swelled to 120 because we didn't want to turn away any children who had auditioned. To keep costs low, we found a mom willing to make costumes. We should have sensed trouble when she felt fried after the first twenty-five. Did we turn down the heat? No way—we just threw more people in the pan and cooked them too. The musical was a great production. The casualty count, though, was high. We've never done a musical since.

Looking back, some might be tempted to claim that the decision to add two shows was the wrong decision. Or maybe that expanding the cast was wrong. Or possibly that making the costumes to save money was a bad choice. And all these observations are somewhat correct. However, the core bad decision was to do the musical at all. This experience is indicative of a problem I see in Promiseland and in ministries elsewhere—the attempt to do too much. I know I must choose to say yes to a reasonable workload that honors God, and no more.

> I must choose to say yes to a reasonable workload that honors God, and no more.

Ministry opportunities always sound so enticing during the initial discussions: More kids. More families. More lives changed. More, more, more! There's nothing wrong with striving to reach an ever increasing number of people for Jesus—fact is, it's what we're supposed to do. The problem occurs when these opportunities are added to a full ministry plate, and nothing is taken off. That plate gets real heavy real fast, and holding it up becomes a strain. God loves anyone who devotes himself to doing his bidding, but he does not want that person to carry an unbearable ministry load. Jesus said in Matthew 11:28, 30, "Come to me, all you who are weary and burdened, and I will give you rest. . . . For my yoke is easy and my burden is light." Isn't it consistent that he wouldn't want us to crush ourselves under the weight of ministry?

The burden is too heavy when there is a routine panic over not knowing how things will get accomplished. The burden is too heavy if projects are abandoned before they're completed so new initiatives can begin. The burden is too heavy when volunteers leave because they feel overworked, resulting in a smaller number to shoulder the weight. When the burden becomes heavy, our attitude tanks, our heart strains, and our call to ministry clouds. This type of workload does not honor God.

To avoid doing damage to yourself, don't be quick to accept fresh initiatives or new requests that are made of you or the whole ministry. Pray about it. Ask other people their opinions—especially your spouse or closest friends who know your current load. If you are a ministry director, gather a team of people who understand the realities of your ministry and think through the costs as well as the benefits together. If the "how" and "who" of an initiative aren't known, then resist the urge to say yes.

Another valuable exercise is to honestly assess whether everything you currently do aligns with your ministry mission, vision, values, strategy, and capacity. And if it doesn't, then be bold and say so. I believe it is more God-honoring to say no or "Only if . . ." in these cases than it is to say yes. Leaders must be willing to say no, but everyone else in the ministry should be willing to ask very direct questions if something doesn't appear reasonably doable. I routinely use this filter when facing attractive opportunities that look like sure winners—such as special events or additional kids' programs. There's nothing wrong with new activities, as long as they align with Promiseland.

To be fair, I realize that in chapter 2 I focused on saying yes. However, there's a big difference between saying yes to a call or new ministry vision from God and agreeing to shoulder more ministry due to the inability to say no—possibly because of tradition or others' expectations. Never forget that *you* will carry whatever load you *agree* to carry. And sometimes simply adding a couple of pounds causes problems. The choice to say yes to a reasonable workload that honors God, and no more, is yours to make.

The right choices for perspective, pace, and load seem like a lot to consider when combined with other ministry goals and objectives. How can one person do it? I don't even try because I'm not in ministry alone.

During physical therapy my family has encouraged me and never let me skip the work to get my knee fit again. They have supported my ministry life in much the same way. My small group and friends have supplied meals following surgery, and they continue to routinely supply joy and counsel. Team members have covered work responsibilities for me and allowed me time to heal. So surround yourself with people you love—people who will walk beside you in good times and tough ones, and who will hold you accountable to live sanely. Surgery and rehabilitation sure opened my eyes to ministry life, and created a fresh desire to do a better job with the choices I make. And now, oh the places I'll go when I can bend my knee 110 degrees. . . .

Until I complete physical therapy, gone are my days of casually jumping into the car and running around town. Life has turned into being careful to simply step over sidewalk cracks. But all that will change, and I will appreciate the rehab road I traveled. You can be sure I'll start to take better care of my knees.

Wherever you are on your ministry journey, make sure that care for your heart and soul is a high priority. This happens when you choose to worship only God, choose to slow down and spend time with God, and choose to say yes to a reasonable workload that honors God. Even Dr. Seuss underscores the value of self-leadership when he says near the end of his book:

> So be sure when you step.
> Step with care and great tact
> And remember that Life's
> A great Balancing Act.[5]

Just make sure you step with boldness—because God is always beside you and wants to help you make great choices. And when that happens, you will finish the adventure stronger than when you began.

In his heart a man plans his course, but the LORD determines his steps.

Proverbs 16:9

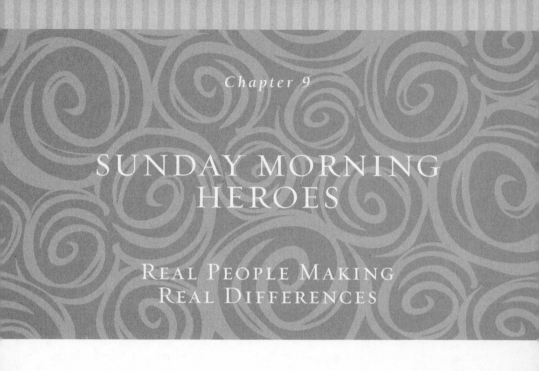

Chapter 9

SUNDAY MORNING HEROES

REAL PEOPLE MAKING REAL DIFFERENCES

At the beginning of the book I shared my love for adventure stories and the characters who live out the action. Regardless of the plot, every tale involves good people and those who are not so good. And somewhere in the cast you'll always find a hero. Everyone loves the hero—especially in real-life stories.

The Bible records several world-changing dramas that involve real heroes. An honor roll appears in Hebrews 11, in which the writer describes an Old Testament hall of fame. These people—from Enoch to Rahab to David—earned their status because they were driven to act based on "assurance of things hoped for, the conviction of things not seen" (v. 1 ESV). In addition to faith, a closer look at heroes reveals that they typically display three additional characteristics.

1. Heroes Excel, Whatever the Circumstances.

Many of the people listed in Hebrews 11 didn't set out to do something noteworthy. Yet they found themselves in extraordinary circumstances in which their responses and actions earned them notoriety. This is also quite often true with more recent heroes.

145

President John F. Kennedy provided an example of modern-day heroics. During World War II, an enemy ship sank his patrol boat, forcing him to swim several miles to shore. While doing so, he towed an injured sailor by clamping the man's life jacket strap in his teeth. Asked later about how he became a hero, he said, "It was easy—they sank my boat."[1] He didn't set out to do anything attention-worthy; he just reacted well to his situation. And more than sixty years later, his feat lives on.

2. Heroes Live Out Their Conviction.

What drives heroes to react the way they do? Typically it's an unwavering conviction to their cause. President Kennedy's cause was the welfare of the men he commanded. Dr. Martin Luther King Jr. is another hero, well-known for his commitment to civil rights. In a letter to a group of very vocal and critical clergymen—penned on paper scraps in a Birmingham, Alabama, jail cell—Dr. King explained why he passionately pursued the cause of equality: "Just as the Apostle Paul left his little village of Tarsus and carried the gospel of Jesus Christ to practically every hamlet and city of the Graeco-Roman world, I too am compelled to carry the gospel of freedom beyond my particular hometown. . . . I cannot sit idly by in Atlanta and not be concerned about what happens in Birmingham."[2]

3. Heroes Rarely Receive Their Due Honor.

Although some heroes enjoy lives decorated with fame for their acts, the majority of them miss out on grand publicity. This reality doesn't diminish the value of their valor—it simply reflects a reality that the limelight has a limited size. That said, the light shines brightly on a very select number of heroes who receive the highest commendation our country offers—the Congressional Medal of Honor. The criteria for this award states that the recipient must "distinguish himself conspicuously by gallantry and intrepidity . . . above and beyond the call of duty."[3] Unfortunately, the majority of individuals who receive the Medal of Honor do not live to receive the award—the price of heroism too often is the person's life. But the conventional battlefield isn't the only place to find individuals worth celebrating.

Look around your ministry today and you will find real-life heroes in your midst. I sure do. When I walk the hallways of Promiseland, I spot people who excel despite challenges, who feel driven by a conviction that kids matter, and who possess no need for recognition. "Above and beyond the call of duty" describes the contributions of many Promiseland staff and volunteers, especially those who have stuck with us through the tough times. They display "gallantry and intrepidity" in their steadfast commitment to reach kids for Jesus—despite my leadership trials and errors. I believe they are the folks who make every word of this book credible. So it's fitting that we end the book by focusing on the people who make any Great Kid-Venture happen in hamlets and cities across the land.

Sunday Morning Heroes

Passion-filled children's ministry workers show up every weekend relatively unnoticed—and churches are fortunate they do, because ministry would quickly wither and drop without them! It's a special person who will rearrange his or her calendar for the chance to make an eternal difference in kids' lives. Their talents could be deployed in a multitude of other venues, but instead they follow a heartbeat from God for children. I call this committed and underrecognized corps "Sunday Morning Heroes." They work in my ministry, in yours, and in churches around the world.

> It's a special person who will rearrange his or her calendar for the chance to make an eternal difference in kids' lives.

I'm so convinced that every children's ministry has heroes in its ranks, that I decided to find a few to highlight during our annual Promiseland Children's Ministry Conference. It was an easy search. Scores of ministries quickly responded to a request for "hero" nominations. I read page after page about people whose individual efforts definitely distinguish them—yet who also represent broad categories of people valiantly serving kids week in and week out. The tough job was selecting only a handful to describe. Their stories stir my heart, and I feel privileged to share them with you.

If you lead people in any capacity, then from the rest of this chapter you can harvest ideas on how to honor people. Specifically, pay close attention to the details about each hero. The leaders who submitted the information know their people well and offered detailed words of affirmation.

After listening to each hero's laurels described during the conference, we invited him or her to come forward onstage. Just imagine the exhilaration these people felt while hearing these comments and watching over four thousand strangers stand to wildly applaud them. And even though the applause was long and from the heart, I have a hunch that the words from their leader touched them most deeply. Who wouldn't enjoy realizing they've been noticed and appreciated?

So as you read these descriptions, consider them thought primers. Picture folks in your ministry who would have made this list if you were the author, and use the page margins to jot down their names. You'll need those names later. And if you wonder whether it's appropriate to call a church worker a hero, remember that Romans 13:7 says we should "pay honor to whom honor is due." So let the honor begin.

Hero #1

Dave Smith, Southside Christian Church, Spokane, Washington

Sunday Morning Heroes are ordinary people whom God uses for extraordinary ministry. Often, the opportunity to serve God with their gifts and talents is the primary motivation that drives them. Our first hero is a large group worship leader whose ministry director describes him as, "a dream come true!" But there's much more to Dave's story—because what sets him apart is not what drives him, it's what he drives. Literally.

Every Saturday evening for more than six years, Dave has traveled to his church. Once there, he has *driven* the church bus home. Dave lives in a pretty tough neighborhood, and going to church is not an option for a lot of kids living around him. So our hero invites any and all children to his house for breakfast on Sunday morning, and then loads everyone into the bus and drives them to church where they attend the children's ministry. On any given weekend, Dave chauffeurs up to twenty kids.

Imagine this hero in action. Think about the chaos he must go through each Sunday morning to feed those kids. Consider the challenge to keep track of them all. But this man sees past all of that to a different picture. He sees kids who need Jesus, who need a better chance at life, who just need someone's helping hand. Dave's ministry director says he has personally escorted at least fifty kids across the line of faith, and that number grows every year.

Dave is called a "dream volunteer" by members of his ministry, and is likely part of some dreams come true for many neighborhood parents. Because of all the worship songs he's led, for the countless pancakes he's made, and on behalf of every child whose road to Jesus began on a bus ride from him, Dave is a Sunday Morning Hero.

Which volunteers in your ministry seem to always look for and reach out to new kids? Who extends ministry past the walls of your church into the community?

Hero #2

Joe Windover, West Gate Chapel, Akron, Ohio

Joe's ministry describes him as "aggressively involved" in behind-the-scenes support. This hero represents all the volunteers who dream up ideas and then work long and usually never-noticed hours to turn them into reality. Joe, and your volunteers just like him, makes sure the room decor feels cool, the stage looks great, and every kid's imagination gets captured. Not a small order—and one that keeps Joe thinking about children's ministry throughout his entire week.

For instance, Joe walks through a hardware store and buys twenty yards of gutter protectors because he reasons, "Hey, our ministry might be able to use this for something." And eventually they do. While others might view a messy garage as an unorganized collection of junk—a shrine to the disposal-challenged—Joe pictures bike helmets, sleds, and broom bristles as bug costumes or some other right-brain creation. Joe's wife, Stacey, says she recognizes a certain look in her husband's eye. "When he asks, 'What do you think?'" she laughs, "I know he really just wants permission to take another home furnishing and use it as a prop."

Joe hit an all-time creative high with an elaborate, "almost-over-the-edge-approach," according to his ministry director, when, as part of a science-themed lesson, he froze bananas and balloons with liquid helium. Along with his intense imagination and creativity, he has earned a reputation for doing everything he can to make others look great. Joe's passion for people shows in a teammate's observation, "He's amazingly encouraging to all of us who serve with him."

A description of King Hezekiah in 2 Chronicles 31:21 says, "And every work that he undertook in the service of the house of God . . . he did with all his heart, and prospered" (ESV). In today's terms, this passage might read, "In his work for God, this guy gives it everything he's got." Regardless of the words, both descriptions describe Joe's heartbeat.

What fuels people like Joe, other than liquid helium? Easy answer. He loves to see the looks on kids' faces as they are swept away learning about God—especially when everything is so cool and so fun that they want to come back to church and learn more. That's the payment that drives him; that's how he prospers. Without a doubt, every work that Joe undertakes in the service of the house of God, he does with all his heart. And for all the out-of-sight efforts that others enjoy but rarely express appreciation for, Joe is a Sunday Morning Hero.

Who in your ministry brings craftsmanship and creativity to work for the kingdom? Which volunteers work hard behind the scenes to set others up for

effective ministry? Who arrives earlier than anyone else when assembly is required—and then stays latest, taking apart all that was assembled?

Hero #3

Becky Swink, River Tree Christian Church, Massillon, Ohio

When children's ministry happens as a team, it can turn into a great hour for big people and kids alike. But just doing ministry work together doesn't guarantee a real sense of teamwork will develop. Oftentimes the secret ingredient that's needed is someone like Becky— radically devoted to reaching kids and sold out to serving volunteers and staff.

Becky represents all the people who provide care to fellow servants, who make sure that others hear words of appreciation, and who ensure people around them receive acts of love. Sometimes this means shepherding other volunteers through difficult times. Other times it involves asking teammates how they are doing, then slowing down to give undivided attention and really listen. Or maybe it's remembering birthdays, going to the hospital, baking cookies, or throwing a party to tell someone, "Thank you for being in our ministry."

In John 13:35 Jesus says, "By this all men will know that you are my disciples, if you love one another." In children's ministry "everyone" includes little sets of eyes that watch how we treat each other. The kind of love that kids need modeled to them is a love so real that they can see it happen. When they watch Becky long enough, they see love in action. When adults step into ministry with her, they feel like they're really on a team.

And that's a feeling that strengthens a ministry. Her ministry director says, "Becky does whatever it takes to make Sunday mornings a success." Because she figured out that success is when people actively love one another, Becky is a Sunday Morning Hero.

Who in your ministry has a reputation for serving teammates? Which person on your team regularly connects with coworkers during nonministry hours?

Hero #4

Cindy Goodspeed, Farmers Branch Church of Christ, Dallas, Texas

Think of the unique sights that those of us who work with children get to enjoy: smiles of two-year-olds, a room of kids singing and doing hand motions to a worship song, children sitting real still and asking Jesus to be their forever friend, and the excited look on a parent's face when his or her child announces that prayer. I wouldn't trade the scenery in children's ministry for anything. Our next hero would love to have that option.

Cindy Goodspeed never enjoys any of these sights because her eyesight is almost totally gone. Imagine doing all the work of children's ministry and not seeing the results. She boldly leads her ministry with a vision she can't see, and with strength that defies reason.

Several years ago, Cindy received a compelling vision for children's ministry, ironically in a church that then had no kids' program. She didn't change or fine-tune a ministry; she created one. And today her vision has become a reality enjoyed by more than three hundred little people who gather each weekend in a new three-million-dollar children's ministry facility! Cindy represents leaders who dream big even when others can't seem to look past the problems at hand.

Cindy pays little attention to her physical challenge because she is on mission to build a prevailing children's ministry. This contagious commitment to a grand purpose compels others to join her—and now a dedicated team of one hundred adults serves those three hundred kids. But it doesn't stop with volunteer recruiting. Her senior pastor says, "On the coattails of God's movement in our children's ministry, our church grew by 33 percent in one eighteen-month period."

152

Cindy approaches ministry in full stride with 1 Samuel 16:7, "Man looks at the outward appearance, but the LORD looks at the heart." Although she can't see the children in her ministry, she focuses on what's needed for little hearts—which I'm convinced mirrors how God views ministry. It also speaks well for her heart, and for those other intensely dedicated leaders throughout the kingdom just like her.

Her pastor goes on to say this about her, "Cindy's eyesight may not always be the liability we think it to be. In many ways, it's an asset because it keeps her radically dependent on the Father for his provision in our children's ministry."

One day in heaven, Cindy will receive even more from God when she finally sees the kids her ministry reached. And the promise of that sight keeps her going year after year. It takes a leader willing to battle very real obstacles to make any children's ministry thrive. And for being exactly that type of leader, Cindy Goodspeed is a Sunday Morning Hero.

Who overcomes obstacles in life to make an impact in your ministry? Do you have a leader who is so committed to reach kids that nothing seems to discourage him or her, at least not for long? Which leader could use some appreciation for beating the odds to help make your ministry prevail?

Hero #5

Ian Jackson, Goodlettsville Cumberland Presbyterian Church, Goodlettsville, Tennessee

To fully appreciate our next hero, imagine life in 1953. A lot of great things started that year. Dr. Jonas Salk announced a new vaccine to prevent polio. Walt Disney's *Peter Pan* opened in a New York theater. A TV series called *The Adventures of Superman* premiered. And speaking of television, the first TV dinners hit the supermarkets.

If you think that this hero was *born* in 1953, then you guessed wrong. That is when Ian *began* as a children's ministry volunteer!

Today he leads a children's small group every Sunday, directs a choir of fourth-, fifth-, and sixth-graders, and helps with a ministry camp and vacation Bible school. His ministry director says, "Despite health complications, Ian is the best volunteer our ministry has ever seen. Ian serves as an incredible role model for kids, parents, volunteers, and me—the children's pastor."

Many people will serve in our ministries for a year because they think they should. Others might do so for a few years during the time the ministry serves their children. Ian represents a portion of an even smaller group—individuals who serve an extraordinary number of years because God specifically called them into a ministry. And it's not just while their kids are in the program, or for a season when it's convenient. This hero distinguishes himself through a lifelong commitment to serve God by serving kids.

When I think of Ian, and all volunteers whose years of service have turned into decades, I remember 2 Chronicles 16:9: "The eyes of the LORD range throughout the earth to strengthen those whose hearts are fully committed to him." It takes strength to serve more than fifty years, so there is no doubt that God has seen Ian's heart for kids—and has known for decades that he is a Sunday Morning Hero.

Who are the veterans in your ministry? Which volunteers have faithfully served kids for many years, or possibly multiple generations of children? If you had a lifetime achievement award to give, whose name(s) would appear on the inscription?

One More Hero

Every Sunday Morning Hero lives out the description of Christian service found in 1 Corinthians 15:58: "Stand firm. Let nothing move you. Always give yourselves fully to the work of the Lord, because you know that your labor in the Lord is not in vain." Holding a baby, singing a song, telling a story, listening to a child, recruiting volunteers, praying for coworkers—none of these are a waste of time because God understands that all of it is done for him.

Every weekend in churches all over the world, heroes inconspicuously walk through the doors. These people excel at what they do because of a conviction that drives them without any expectation of honor. They might not realize it or admit it, but they are heroes nonetheless—to coworkers, to parents, and to kids. And if you care enough about your ministry to read this entire book, then I suspect you might be one, too.

> If you care enough about your ministry to read this entire book, then I suspect you might be a hero, too.

In today's world, it's easy to be too busy to volunteer or too distracted by a career to answer God's call into children's ministry. Thanks for saying yes to serving kids. You willingly traded the easy way for an exciting journey. As God watches you embark on your own action story, know that he promises your award waits for you at the end of your ministry adventure. And until that day comes, know that in my book *you* are a Sunday Morning Hero!

Hero #6

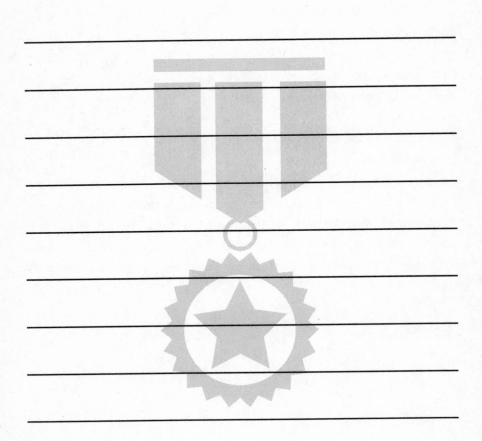

This page is intentionally blank so *you* can write in the name of a special person in your ministry and a description of their heroic contribution. Then give this book to that person. Consider doing this for each of the people whose names or faces came to mind as you read the last chapter. Imagine how delighted your team members will be to read this book, turn to this page, and see their names and your words of affirmation. Remember, heroes rarely receive the honor due them—so this is your chance to let the honor begin!

A FINAL WORD

This book began with two key questions. The first asked, "What is going on?" in children's ministries that have dared to make significant changes and then gone on to prosper and prevail. You have, no doubt, found the answers to that question in the nine chapters you read. But I hope you have more than just a clear picture of what God has done in these thriving ministries. This book's intent is to spark your own undeniable passion to see your ministry become the best hour of every kid's week.

The second question asked, "Could it happen in your church?" Theoretically, of course, that is absolutely possible. Promiseland changed, as have thousands of other children's ministries around the world. But theory alone isn't enough. Maybe a better way to phrase the question is, "Will it happen in your church?" Or if it does, "Will you be part of it?" And I can't answer either question—only you can. But I do pray that you will dream big for your ministry and for your role, and remember that God "is able to do immeasurably more than all we ask or imagine" (Eph. 3:20).

In chapter 1 we looked at a group of Bible heroes woven together by their faith. But faith in what? Hebrews 11:13 tells us that each of them had faith in a vision for what God wanted to accomplish. And then they made themselves available for his purposes. Just a few pages ago we saw a group of modern-day Sunday Morning Heroes living a similar life. And maybe a fresh list, written years from now, awaits your name:

By faith, (your name) held babies year after year and offered prayers for little ones that heaven could not ignore. By faith, (your name) led and loved a rowdy small group of fifth-graders and helped them believe that God has a purpose for their lives. By faith, (your name) abandoned lifelong career aspirations to work full-time in children's ministry, based only on a nudge from God that lost kids needed to be found. By faith, (your name) cast a new ministry vision and kept chasing that vision with a team that kept going even when faced with skepticism and opposition.

The bottom line is that your response to all you've read will determine whether or not another new Great Kid-Venture story will start in your ministry. And the faith-filled choice to participate in what God wants to accomplish is yours alone. Will you try to make it happen in your church or be part of the adventure going on already—yes or no? Pick one answer and write it in the box below. Because the final word that really counts in this book isn't mine—it's *yours*.

PERSONAL EXERCISES AND TEAM EXPERIENCES

I am always amazed at how much serving in ministry helps me grow and change as an individual Christ-follower. The personal exercises that follow are designed to help you do the same. Before you meet as a team, take time to process new ideas and insights individually—a step that will open up all kinds of possibilities for your group to have animated and lively discussions.

After the personal exercises, you will find ideas for crafting meaningful experiences for your team (key leaders in the ministry). Gone are the days when groups of people just sit in a circle and discuss questions. Today's ministry teams, especially those interested in a ministry adventure, deserve more. The setting and activities planned for a meeting can contribute as much to a successful outcome as the topic and questions—even more so with newer teams.

Chapter 1

Personal Exercise

Read Hebrews 11:1–2, 6. Notice how faith is required in order to follow God. Spend a few minutes thinking about the following:

1. How has God been faithful to you in the past? Be specific as you recount blessings and provision.
2. God wants us to fill our minds with his promises to encourage us along the way.

Read through the five promises from chapter 1:

- With faith in God, all things are possible. He is smart enough, strong enough, and definitely has a plan (Matt. 19:26).
- He will provide all that's needed when a God-honoring vision is pursued (John 14:14).

- There is strength in working together (Eccl. 4:9–10, 12).
- God is in control even when everything feels out of control (Rom. 8:28).
- He definitely has plans for you (Jer. 29:11).

Which of the promises do you need to hang onto right now? Based on your choice, how does God want to grow your faith at this moment? Which promise do you think your ministry needs to be reminded of as you move into a new day together?

Close this personal time in prayer, telling God you are ready to start on a new adventure with him. Ask him to grow your faith in things you do not yet "see." Thank him for the promises he gives to encourage and guide us. Pray that your children's ministry will become all God wants it to be.

Team Experience

The leader of this exercise reads an adventure story from a favorite children's book or shows a short movie clip as the team begins their time together. The leader shares what he or she learned from the book or movie adventure and then gives each person three minutes to tell one of their favorite adventure stories and what they learned from it. This activity will help build community on your team. Discuss the positive experiences that come when you embark on an adventure, as well as the potential negative things that can happen when venturing into the unknown.

Next, have a team member read Hebrews 11:1–2, 6. Ask each person:

- How do you feel about the Great Kid-Venture going on in your ministry right now?
- Is the idea of making your ministry more effective exciting to you?
- Are you personally ready for a faith adventure, and is the ministry ready for one?

Now create a visual aid to remind the team of God's trustworthiness.

A. Give each person a standard index card and ask him or her to write one truth about God that tells why he can be trusted. For instance, one card might say, "God is all-powerful" or "God is all-knowing." Everyone then takes turns sharing what they wrote and why they believe God can be trusted.

B. Tape all the cards up on a poster board for everyone to see.

C. Write the five promises listed in the personal exercise on index cards and tape them on the poster board.

D. Give each team member a colored sticker to place on the promise they believe your ministry needs most.

See if any common themes emerge from the group by looking at the promises that have the most stickers on them. Wrap up by acknowledging that this meeting is just a first step toward addressing the challenges you face as a ministry. Affirm everyone's contribution.

Close in prayer, thanking God for being trustworthy, praising him for keeping his promises, and asking him to grow your faith as a team and provide the wisdom you will need for the adventure ahead.

Suggestion to Leader — Start a notebook or scrapbook that records your team's experiences along the way. You can add a different page after every team experience, to remind your team of the work they have done to make your ministry more effective. Books like this are a great way to affirm and celebrate your team. To start, write the words "The Great Kid-Venture" on a poster board and have each member of the team sign it. Take a photo of the team holding this sign. Use this picture and the index cards from your team experience to create the first chapter of your scrapbook. If you'd like, come up with a chapter title — one that best captures your team at the outset of this adventure.

Chapter 2

Personal Exercise

Read Hebrews 11:3, focusing on the words "so that what is seen was not made out of what was visible."

Consider for a moment that God made something out of nothing. God has the power to speak words and bring the whole universe into existence. This truth gives us great encouragement for days when we feel like we have no courage. Our God has the power to give us courage—to create something out of nothing—so our souls are calm and peaceful. God invites us to tell him what we need.

Spend some time telling God what you need today. Maybe it's something new like courage. Or perhaps you need to let go of something that is distracting you from God?

Now focus on your ministry, because God can help you create a new picture of it. Even if there are parts missing in your ministry scene today, God has the power to make an invisible dream clear to see in his timing.

Write down your answers to these questions:

What do you think your children's ministry is doing really well today?
In what ways could it do a better job and be more effective?
What would ministry look like if *everything* were working right?
What would draw even more kids to your church?
What would help give volunteers an optimal serving experience?
What would a great volunteer team look like?
How would you describe your dream facility?

Bring your responses to your next team experience.

Close your personal time by praying for your ministry's future. Ask God to help you let go of the past and say, "Yes!" to a more effective future reaching kids. Pray for him to energize your team experience as each member shares his or her dreams. Ask God to increase your team's faith, knowing he has the power you need for whatever lies ahead.

Team Experience

Build community by asking each person to share how he or she came to your church and became involved in your children's ministry. Discuss as a group what might have happened if each team member had not followed God's leading—and what you would be missing as a team.

Ask someone to read Hebrews 11:8–10. In these verses we learn that Abraham was asked to obey God and leave his home, a place that was safe and familiar to him, and go to another land. And we read that because of his faith in God, Abraham obeyed and went—even though he didn't know where he was going to end up. Now that's an example of a real faith adventure! Are we willing to obey and follow God just like Abraham?

Next, create a visual representation of your ministry and its vision.

- Ask everyone to write on yellow Post-It notes the things that are going well in your ministry. Invite individuals to share what they wrote with a brief explanation and put their Post-It note on a poster board. Title this category "Ministry Today."

- After each team member has shared, give a roll of Lifesavers candy to everyone, thanking them and affirming their contribution to your ministry. Their faithfulness has taken your ministry this far. Kids will be in heaven one day because of their love, their prayers, and their obedience to God.

- Arrange the yellow Post-It notes into the shape of a smiling face to represent the truth that God is pleased with the way team members have faithfully served kids at your church.

- Now, using green Post-It notes, ask everyone to write suggestions for how your ministry could become more effective each week.

- Invite each member to share what he or she wrote with a brief explanation. Keep the conversation focused on how the ministry might grow in reaching more kids, rather than letting this time become a gripe session.

- Place the green Post-It notes on a poster board titled "We Could Grow."
- Finally, ask everyone to write his or her ministry dream ideas for the future on blue Post-It notes, keeping in mind these questions:

  What does our ministry look like when everything is working right?
  How could we best serve kids each weekend?
  How could we provide the optimal serving experience for our volunteers?
  What would our ideal facility look like?
  How many lost kids would we be reaching?
  Tell the group to remember that this is an ideal picture of your future together, so dream big! God has the power to turn our invisible dreams into something visible that will help us serve kids better (Hebrews 11:3).

- Invite team members to share what they wrote with a brief explanation and then place their blue Post-It notes (for blue-sky ideas) in the shape of a V on a poster board titled "Our Ministry Dream."
- These ideas form the new vision for your ministry. Look at what your ministry can become, with God's help in the future. Isn't that picture exciting?

Close this team exercise by praying together that God will give you all the faith you need to say yes to a new vision. Ask for courage to face the unknown adventure that lies ahead.

Suggestion to Leader — Mark the moment by taking a picture of the team by the blue V. Save all the Post-It notes from these exercises and the photo for your team notebook or scrapbook. Create your own chapter title that best suits your team's journey together.

Chapter 3

Personal Exercise

Read Hebrews 11:1–31. Consider how many different individuals God used to accomplish his work. Do you realize God has chosen you to play a role in shaping the future of your ministry? Just think about how many new kids could be impacted as you move toward greater effectiveness. God has plans to use your gifts, life experiences, and character to accomplish his work. He has great plans to use you in his adventure story at your church.

Reflect on why you are serving in children's ministry. As your team moves into a new future together, what role do you see yourself playing? Which ministry activities fill you up, and which ones drain you?

Write your answer to this question: With which person in Hebrews 11 do you most identify? Why?

Close this time in prayer, thanking God for choosing you to be a part of his adventure. Worship him as the Creator who made you just the way you are. Ask him to use you, protect you from sin, and grow your character so you will act more and more like his Son, Jesus, every day.

Team Experience

Enjoy a meal or snack together as a team. Build community by asking members to share what gives them the most joy when they serve in ministry. Then ask people to talk about what drains their joy in ministry. Let everyone share the role they would like to play in the future.

Ask each person to share which person from Hebrews 11 they most identify with. Ask why they chose that particular person. Close this part of the meeting by affirming the differences and unique contributions each member brings to the team, noting that a team with complementary skills is needed to help your ministry achieve its mission.

Now focus on your ministry's mission statement. Ask the team whether or not they think your ministry has a clear mission to accomplish. Bring out the yellow, green, and blue Post-It notes from the chapter 2 team experience. Allow time for a lengthy discussion of these important questions:

What will success look like in our ministry?

What do we want to be true of kids when they graduate from our ministry?

Does our ministry mission statement align with our church's mission?

Do you need to revise your mission statement? Do you need to create one? If so, the following five-step exercise can help you do just that. This exercise blends individual work with team sessions and should be completed over the course of a few weeks, or months if needed. Allow plenty of time to fully discuss the spectrum of ideas sure to surface in each step. Set a deadline, though, to keep the team focused on the goal of completing the exercise.

- *Step 1: Create*

  Complete the following two statements individually.

  As a children's ministry, we want to . . . (do what?)

  So that . . . (what happens as a result?)

- *Step 2: Consolidate*

  Meet as a team and invite everyone to share their answers from step 1. Record all responses so everyone can see each person's input. Circle the most commonly used words and phrases. Discuss the unique items to clarify meaning and decide whether to include them or not.

- *Step 3: Craft*

  As a team, begin to draft potential mission statements, using the agreed-upon words from step 2. To start, don't be overly concerned with length, so all concepts are represented—you are very likely to have two sentences. Then try to combine them into one statement, eliminating redundant words.

- *Step 4: Compare*

  Refer to your church's mission statement, if you have one. Are the two mission statements similar? Do they sound as if they come from the same church body? Make any necessary adjustments.

- *Step 5: Complete*

  Edit your wording with the intent to make the statement easy to remember. This will likely involve eliminating or changing words. Consider asking people not previously involved for their ideas, especially someone with strong communication skills and experience in ministry or the marketplace. Once you've created your mission statement, be sure to get the approval of your senior leadership.

Now that you have your mission statement, it's time to evaluate your ministry activities and programming to see how everything aligns. What do you need to continue doing? What do you need to stop? What should you start doing to maximize your potential? Go back through your Post-It notes to remind you of your earlier thinking on this topic.

When your mission statement is completed and you are clear on what you are going to say yes or no to as a team, set aside time to mark the moment. An idea for this special time came from a Willow Creek Community Church groundbreaking ceremony.

- Schedule an outside gathering for your team. When everyone arrives, give each person a three-foot wooden stake (available at hardware stores).
- Each person then attaches a strip of colored plastic flagging ribbon (also available at hardware stores), about eighteen inches in length, to the end of the stake.
- Ask everyone to write your ministry's mission statement on the side of his or her stake. Invite them to sign their names on it and add a Bible verse that is significant to them.
- Then hand out hammers and, all at the same time, drive your stakes into the ground as a reminder of your commitment to your mission.

- Finally, end by praying together. Thank God for the different skills and unique contributions of each team member that make your ministry possible.

Suggestion to Leader—Take a photo of your team and their stakes. Add this to your scrapbook with a printed statement of your ministry mission. Leave the stakes in the ground for a time and periodically visit this special place to celebrate how God is helping you achieve your mission.

Chapter 4

Personal Exercise

Read Hebrews 11:32–38. Isn't it amazing how committed these people were to achieving the mission God gave them? They were willing to do anything God asked them. How are you doing in the area of willingness? Take a moment to consider whether you need to grow in this area and if so, ask God to help you.

Consider what kids experience when they come to your program each week. Think about how your ministry is doing in reaching kids—specifically, what values do you have that influence how you meet kids' needs? Should any values be added to your present list in order to help you become more effective? Should any values be taken off your list? Do you have a list?

Write your thoughts and be ready to share them with your team.

Close your personal time by letting God know that you want to have the boldness and endurance of the men and women in Hebrews 11.

Team Experience

Take your team on a field trip to a local place that kids love such as a toy store, a bookstore, a restaurant, or a theme park.

Invite your team to walk around the location and observe all the ways kids are served.

- What does this place do well?
- What can the team learn from this establishment? For instance, what safety precautions do they take and are they effective?
- How do they attract new kids and keep regulars coming back? Try to list the establishment's values.
- Give your team an allotted amount of time to observe, and then gather them back together to discuss what they learned.
- Have someone record comments, and finish by taking a creative team photograph to remember your field trip.

Next, find a quiet spot to sit as a team and talk about your ministry values. Do you have your own set of values? What are they? Are they the right ones to help you achieve your mission? Pull out your yellow, green, and blue Post-It notes for review. See if together you can gain agreement on what your values should be for your ministry. Try to emerge from this discussion with a list of values. Then discuss how you will effectively implement these values each weekend. What will have to change? What is the right time frame in which these changes should occur? How will your values be communicated throughout the ministry?

Close by praying together specifically for the lost kids in your neighborhoods, those who are still far from God's family. Pray that God will use your values to create a ministry that kids love so much that will literally drag their parents to church. Ask God to draw them to your ministry and bring them across the line of faith.

Suggestion to Leader — Add to your scrapbook the photo, the comments from the field trip, and a finished list of your values. Remember to create your own unique title for this chapter, one that best reflects your team's adventure together.

Chapter 5

Personal Exercise

Read Hebrews 11, paying attention to how the individuals were spiritually gifted. Some were visionary leaders, and others were military commanders brimming with strategy. Nehemiah was an administrator, while Elisha was a prophet. The body of Christ has great diversity and variety when it comes to spiritual gifts. God uses all of them and doesn't value one gift above another.

You too have a unique blend of spiritual gifts that were given to you to be used for the good of the body of Christ. Think about your giftedness. Check the appendixes at the back of this book to review a list of spiritual gifts. Which gifts do you think you have? Are you using your spiritual gifts optimally right now? Do you feel you are serving in a role that matches your gifts?

Close your time by thanking God for the gifts he has given you. Ask him to show you how to steward them wisely, using them to accomplish his work in this world.

Team Experience

Ask someone to make a homemade appetizer or dessert to bring to the meeting. When the group arrives, spend some time building community as you eat. Then ask each person to tell about his or her favorite appetizer or dessert. Have they ever tried to cook something and forgotten to add an ingredient? Have they ever put in too much of one ingredient by mistake? No doubt you will hear some funny stories around your circle.

God knows how critical it is for us to have the right mix of spiritual gifts in our ministry so we serve our kids well. Ask team members to share what they believe their spiritual gifts are. Invite the group to give feedback to each person regarding how they have seen them use their gifts in your ministry. Are team members serving in roles that match their spiritual giftedness? Discuss the rest of your volunteers—are they aware of their spiritual gifts and are they in the best roles?

Next, look at the rest of your ministry strategy, especially your curriculum and creative programming. Are your values represented by how you serve kids each Sunday? Would it help to move toward a large-group-and-small-group strategy? If so, how would you do it? If not, what else might work?

Make a list of the changes you want to address and prioritize the items. Discuss which changes can be made in the next thirty days, ninety days, six months, and one year. Remember that a good place to start is establishing your own four sets of eyes. Identify any other roles you feel might be critical along the way.

Close your time by reading 1 Corinthians 12:4–31 and praying. Thank God for the diversity of gifts and skills on your team. Pray for the roles/spiritual gifts you're waiting for him to fill. Tell God how you appreciate being brought together to serve in his kingdom.

Suggestion to Leader — Take a photo of your team that illustrates their dependence on each other. They might build a pyramid, link arms, or stack all their hands on top of each others'. Place the photo in your scrapbook along with the prioritized list of changes you want to address.

Chapter 6

Personal Exercise

When we read Hebrews 11:32, we realize that there were other heroes of the faith—too many for the writer to mention them all.

Nehemiah is not listed but had quite a story, which hits a crescendo with this passage: "So the wall was completed on the twenty-fifth of Elul, in fifty-two days. When all our enemies heard about this, all the surrounding nations were afraid and lost their self-confidence, because they realized that this work had been done with the help of our God" (Neh. 6:15–16).

Think for a moment about Nehemiah. He was wild about the assignment God had given him. He was passionate about rebuilding the walls around Jerusalem, a pretty impossible task. In reading how he accomplished his mission, several things are clear. First, he was a man of prayer. He was clear that the work would only get finished with the "help of our God." Second, he put together a plan that would allow him to organize the people to get the work done. Third, Nehemiah was a motivator who could rally his workers to action.

Now spend time praying for the volunteers in your ministry. Thank God for the faithful volunteers you already have. Ask for his help in recruiting new people with a heart to serve kids. Ask God to help you be a person wild about your ministry vision.

Team Experience

Make five copies of the baseball on page 173.

Play a tape of a motivational speaker who is compelling and convincing at articulating vision. You could use a clip of one of our presidents, past or present. Or maybe Martin Luther King Jr.'s "I Have a Dream" speech. Discuss what you like about the speaker—was he or she wild about the topic? How could you tell?

Now focus on your ministry. Read Nehemiah 6:15–16. Recruiting new volunteers can often feel like an impossible task for all of us. Discuss lessons the team notices from Nehemiah's example.

Discuss the team's passion for the ministry's vision. Then share ideas for addressing these questions:

Do the people in your church know how significant your ministry is to your church's mission?

What kind of reputation do you think you have with other volunteers and with your church body? What do you need to improve?

Next, on each of the baseballs write the name of an audience segment in your church (each audience is discussed in chapter 6). The list includes: Everybody, Special-Event Volunteers, 1:6 Adult Volunteers, Every-Week Volunteers, Core Volunteers. Offer ideas for how you will cast vision to each audience, and write those ideas on the corresponding baseballs. Allow plenty of time to brainstorm and record your answers.

Close by praying for the people represented by each ball, asking God to help you hit a home run with each audience.

Suggestion to Leader — Give everyone a baseball hat, possibly have several hold a baseball bat, and take a photo together. Place the photo and the baseballs with your recruiting ideas on them in your scrapbook. Remember to create an original chapter title that best reflects your team.

Chapter 7

Personal Exercise

In Hebrews 11:11 we are reminded of Abraham and Sarah's story. Read their account in Genesis 18. What seemed a preposterous idea became an incredible miracle. God came through in his own timing, and the couple became parents just as he said they would.

Reflect for a moment—have you ever felt it was a preposterous hope to have a core of volunteers who feel valued, connected, included, and challenged? Do you ever feel it will take ninety years for you to get there?

On a deeply personal level, what are you waiting on God for these days? When you think about your own journey in your ministry, what has your experience been like? Have you been waiting a long time for someone to value the role you play? Have you ever felt disconnected and alone? Have you been waiting a long time to be included in the information loop? Are you feeling stagnant in your current role? Are you nursing any hurt feelings or grudges toward anyone from your ministry? Is there anyone with whom you need to resolve conflict?

Close your personal time with prayer. Ask God to give you the patience you need to wait for his timing, and the faith to take action when the time is here.

Team Experience

For this meeting, photocopy and enlarge the four pictures of the ministry monsters and their monologues from chapter 7.

To continue the theme, bring a monster-sized snack or dinner that you can enjoy together—possibly a giant cookie, deep-dish pizza, or party-size sub sandwich.

Start your community-building time by asking each person to share one "huge" positive aspect people enjoy about volunteerism in your ministry. Let each member share one "big" reason why he or she enjoys serving on this team. Record the comments to save for your scrapbook.

Now focus on the four ministry monsters. Put their pictures up in a visible place. Start with the first monster, Used and Abused. Ask one of your team members to read the monologue aloud, and then ask everyone if this monster has gained any ground with your volunteers. If so, how? What things do you need to change to kick this monster out? Give everyone Post-It notes to write down ways your ministry can value volunteers, and stick these notes on the monster's picture. Follow the same steps with the other three monsters.

Close your time by praying together. Ask God to help you honor and value volunteers. Pray that he will give you patience to wait on his timing and faith to take action when the time is right. Tell God about your belief that the answer is, "No!" to the question in Genesis 18:14, "Is anything too hard for the LORD?"

Suggestion to Leader — Mark the moment by taking a photo of your volunteers holding up the four monster pictures with Post-Its stuck on them. Have everyone pose doing a kick toward the camera — signifying the team's desire to kick all the monsters out of your ministry.

Chapter 8

Personal Exercise

Read Hebrews 11:6. This verse tells us that God doesn't want us to just believe that he exists; he wants us to earnestly seek him.

He desires a personal relationship that changes our lives. And the change he wants is ongoing.

The exercise below gives you the opportunity to fill out your own prescription for change. Place a check mark next to the area that needs your attention and God's help. Consider using this exercise as your annual physical, returning to this page for a check-up every twelve months.

Worship only God

- How can I grow in my relationship with God?
- Where do I need to take a next step in the months ahead when it comes to the perspective of my life?
- When do I spend time alone with God?
- When do I regularly attend services where I worship God and am fed spiritually?
- What situations produce anxiety or fear in me? What is the root cause of those reactions, and is ill-placed worship a factor?
- When do I deliberately, although cleverly, seek to position myself to be noticed and receive praise?

Slow down and spend time with God

- List your personal priorities on paper. Fill in the number of hours needed to fulfill all these priorities. Now see if you can fit the ministry responsibilities you've committed to. Be realistic! Does it all even fit in one week? Where have you overcommitted? Determine what is realistic and what must be eliminated, and how you will do it.
- Am I doing things each week that fill me up spiritually? Like studying God's Word, journaling, taking walks in nature, spending time in solitude, reading books, listening to worship CDs?

Say yes to a reasonable workload that honors God, and no more

- Who in my life knows me well enough to hold me accountable to living sanely? Is it a small group? A mentor? Is a counselor an option to be explored?
- Do I spend the majority of my time exercising my giftedness?
- If not, what needs to change, or who needs to know about this to help make necessary changes?
- Identify the responsibilities you have that feel heavy, and develop specific ideas about how to ease that feeling. Can a task be reassigned, or delayed for a season? Whose help do you need to make this happen?

Now determine the next steps you need to take to guard your heart. You might find it helpful to share what you learned with a trusted friend who will hold you accountable in the areas you identified in your prescription. Agree to future dates when you can meet and check on your progress.

Close your personal time in prayer. Start by thanking God for all of his blessings to you. Ask for his help so you can love him first and foremost. This requires confessing any areas of sin and asking for his forgiveness. Praise him for who he is. Tell him you want Christ to be more fully formed in you.

Team Experience

Meet in a place with exercise equipment of any type. Start your time building community by asking each person to share about the piece of exercise equipment they believe is most needed in their spiritual life right now. Then ask everyone to share what area of self-leadership they struggle with most—perspective, pace, or load.

Discuss any common themes. As a ministry team, is there something to which you all need to pay attention? Be sure to talk about solutions. How is the fun level on your team? Do you ever play together and just have a good time?

Ask each person how the team can support him or her in the weeks ahead. To encourage and support one another, it's important to know what each teammate considers helpful. Set a date to revisit this discussion as a team to check on progress.

Next, read Psalm 23 together. Then pray for each other, asking God to restore, refresh, and refuel each team member.

End this experience by taking your team to a place to have fun together. See a funny movie, go out for lunch, play on a playground—do whatever it takes for your team to laugh and enjoy themselves.

Suggestion to Leader —Take a photo as you're having fun, as a reminder to guard your heart while doing ministry together. Add to your scrapbook the photo and a picture of a big red heart with Proverbs 14:30 ("A heart at peace gives life to the body") written on it. Create a chapter title that captures your team's experiences in your journey together.

Chapter 9

Personal Exercise

If you received this book from your ministry leader, he or she may have included a hero description about you at the end of chapter 9.

Using your leader's description and those in chapter 9 as examples, write a one-paragraph description about each of your teammates, telling them why you believe they are Sunday Morning Heroes. Affirm their service, their character, and the unique contributions they bring to your team. Be prepared to share your descriptions during the team experience.

End your personal time by praying for each of your team members. Thank God for each person on your team and the chance to experience this adventure together. Pray that God will use the words you wrote to encourage your teammates.

Team Experience

Choose to have this meeting in a comfortable, informal environment that is quiet enough for everyone to easily hear one another. Perhaps a cozy family room in a team member's home. When everyone is settled, read aloud from chapter 9 the three paragraphs in the section called "One More Hero." Select one person from the team and ask all of your teammates to read why they think this person is a

Sunday Morning Hero. Do this for each person around your circle. This will be a very emotional time for your team. People love to hear how they have made a difference when they use their gifts to serve. It really ministers to them in a deep way, so be sure to stress the importance of everyone participating.

Close by praying together. Thank God for how far you have come as a team. Offer praise to him for all you have learned. Voice your worship to him for all the prayers he has answered along the way. Tell him that you want to "stand firm," "let nothing move you," and "always give yourselves fully to the work of the Lord" (1 Corinthians 15:58) until the job is done. Promise to keep trusting him and taking leaps of faith—knowing that he is the author of your Great Kid-Venture.

Suggestion to Leader —Take one additional photo together. You decide the pose for this one. Add the photo to your scrapbook with the words "Sunday Morning Heroes" written above the photo. Include 1 Corinthians 15:58. Create your own original chapter title that best reflects your team's experiences together on the journey thus far. Great job — way to go!

APPENDIX A

Mission Statements Based on the Great Commission
(Chapter 3)

The Great Commission (Matthew 28:19–20)	Willow Creek Community Church	Promiseland Ministry Mission
"Therefore go and make disciples of all nations . . .	To turn irrelegious people . . .	To supplement the family in reaching kids . . .
. . . teaching them to obey everything I have commanded you."	. . . into fully devoted followers of Christ.	. . . and helping them become fully devoted followers of Christ.

Indicators of Spiritual Maturity—The Five Gs
(Chapter 3)

Grace (Romans 3:23–24)

Every kid should understand that there is a gift of grace needed by all people, have the opportunity to respond, and receive encouragement to share this gift with others.

Growth (Colossians 2:6–7)

Kids' faith should cause them to change from the inside out, with this change evident to others.

Groups (Mark 3:14; Acts 2:46)

All people share a common need to feel connected. Small groups serve as a safe setting for spiritual growth.

Gifts (1 Corinthians 12)

All Christians receive spiritual gifts/talents that they are expected to use in the work of a local body of believers. And it's never too early to start helping people discover their giftedness.

Good Stewardship (Malachi 3:10; Mark 12:41–44)

Everything we have belongs to God, so it honors him for us to manage resources wisely and give them away generously.

APPENDIX B

The Ten Core Values of Willow Creek Community Church
(Chapter 4)

Value One   **We believe that anointed teaching is the catalyst for transformation in individuals' lives and in the church.**
This includes the concept of teaching for life-change (Romans 12:7; 2 Timothy 3:16–17; James 1:23–25).

Value Two   **We believe that lost people matter to God, and therefore ought to matter to the church.**
This includes the concepts of relational evangelism and evangelism as a process (Luke 5:30–32; 15:1–32; Matthew 18:4).

Value Three   **We believe that the church should be culturally relevant while remaining doctrinally pure.**
This includes the concept of sensitively relating to our culture through our facility, printed materials, and use of the arts (1 Corinthians 9:19–23).

Value Four   **We believe that Christ-followers should manifest authenticity and yearn for continuous growth.**
This includes the concepts of personal authenticity, character, and wholeness (Ephesians 4:25–26, 32; Hebrews 12:1; Philippians 1:6).

Value Five   **We believe that a church should operate as a unified community of servants with men and women stewarding their spiritual gifts.**
This includes the concepts of unity, servanthood, spiritual gifts, and ministry callings (1 Corinthians 12; 14; Romans 12; Ephesians 4; Psalm 133:1).

Value Six **We believe that loving relationships should permeate every aspect of church life.**
This includes the concepts of love-driven ministry, ministry accomplished in teams, and relationship building
(1 Corinthians 13; Nehemiah 3; Luke 10:1; John 13:34–35).

Value Seven **We believe that life-change happens best in small groups.**
This includes the concepts of discipleship, vulnerability, and accountability (Luke 6:12–13; Acts 2:44–47).

Value Eight **We believe that excellence honors God and inspires people.**
This includes the concepts of evaluation, critical review, intensity, and excellence (Colossians 3:17; Malachi 1:6–14; Proverbs 27:17).

Value Nine **We believe that churches should be led by men and women with leadership gifts.**
This includes the concepts of empowerment, servant leadership, strategic focus, and intentionality (Nehemiah 1–2; Romans 12:8; Acts 6:2–5).

Value Ten **We believe that the pursuit of full devotion to Christ and his cause is normal for every believer.**
This includes the concepts of stewardship, servanthood, downward mobility, and the pursuit of kingdom goals
(1 Kings 11:4; Philippians 2:1–11; 2 Corinthians 8:7).

Six Core Ministry Values

(Chapter 4)

Value One

Promiseland Is Child-Targeted (1 Corinthians 9:22).

Value Two

Promiseland Is Safe (Mark 10:14).

Value Three

Promiseland Teaching Is Relevant and Application-Oriented (Psalm 119:11).

Value Four

Promiseland Will Teach the Bible Creatively.

Value Five

Promiseland Will Intentionally Shepherd in Small Groups (2 Timothy 2:2; Acts 2:42–47).

Value Six

Promiseland Is Fun!

APPENDIX C

A Typical Hour in Promiseland
(Chapter 5)

Volunteer Team Huddles (45 minutes before start)

A brief meeting in which the leader reinforces ministry vision, provides important information, and gives the team an opportunity to pray for the hour and for each other.

Activity Stations (30 minutes before start)

Features table games, crafts, and other fun activities. This is unstructured time labeled "play with a purpose." Small group leaders use this opportunity to build relationships with kids. Establishes an atmosphere of fun.

Kid Connection (first 10 minutes)

Small groups briefly meet to reestablish community with one another and answer a question or two designed to focus them on the lesson to follow.

Large Group Time (next 20 minutes)

All groups gather in a common area for a Bible lesson that is interactive, life-changing, engaging, and fun enough to keep each child's full attention.

Small Group Time (final 30 minutes)

Children connect back with the groups they were in during Kid Connection to creatively discover and discuss ways they can apply the Bible truth learned in Large Group. This is the ideal setting for intentional shepherding by the adult small group leader.

Spiritual Gifts

(Chapter 5)

Administration

Ability to organize people, tasks, or events to accomplish ministry effectively and efficiently.

Apostleship

Ability to start and oversee new churches or ministries.

Craftsmanship

Ability to design or construct items for ministry.

Creative Communication

Ability to communicate God's truth through a variety of art forms.

Discernment

Ability to distinguish between truth and error, various motives, or the presence of evil.

Encouragement

Ability to present truth to strengthen and comfort those who are wavering.

Evangelism

Ability to effectively communicate the gospel in a compelling way.

Faith

Ability to act on God's promises with confidence and unwavering belief.

Giving

Ability to contribute resources with great cheerfulness and liberality.

Healing

Ability to be God's means for moving people toward wholeness.

Helps (Serving)

Ability to joyfully accomplish practical tasks that serve others and support ministry.

Hospitality

Ability to joyfully create an environment that welcomes others and puts them at ease.

Intercession

Ability to consistently and passionately pray on behalf of others.

Interpretation

Ability to make known the message given by one speaking in tongues.

Knowledge

Ability to bring crucial truth to the body of Christ through biblical insight and understanding.

Leadership

Ability to cast vision, motivate, and direct people to collectively accomplish the purposes of God.

Mercy

Ability to cheerfully and practically help those who are suffering.

Miracles

Ability to authenticate ministry through supernatural actions that glorify Christ.

Prophecy

Ability to relevantly proclaim truth in a way that exposes sin and prompts conviction and repentance.

Shepherding

Ability to nurture and guide people toward spiritual maturity.

Teaching

Ability to clearly explain God's truth and inspire growth in Christ-followers.

Tongues

Ability to speak or pray in an unknown language.

Wisdom

Ability to apply spiritual insight to specific issues, often in the midst of conflict or confusion.[1]

APPENDIX D

Promiseland Curriculum

Transform your outdated Sunday school program into a thriving Children's Ministry! Promiseland Curriculum creatively teaches biblical truths in large groups and models caring community in small groups. The lessons are sequenced in a two year cycle for three grade levels and provide six years of fun, relevant biblical teaching for kids in kindergarten through fifth grade. With this reusable, reproducible curriculum, you'll never have to worry about what to teach next Sunday, next quarter, or next year!

Two Year Cycle:
- God's Story: Genesis—Revelation
- Doing Life with God in the Picture

Three Grade Levels:
- Kindergarten and First grade
- Second and Third grade
- Fourth and Fifth grade

Three Quarterly Kits with Thirteen Lessons:
- Fall quarter: September—November
- Winter quarter: December—February
- Spring quarter: March—May

Large Group / Small Group Format:
- Activity Stations   During arrival
- Kid Connection in Small Groups   5 minutes
- Large Group Worship & Bible Lesson   30 minutes
- Small Group Discussion & Shepherding   25 minutes

Promiseland Curriculum is available through Willow Creek Resources, Zondervan Church**Source**, and Christian book stores. Additional resources and support can be found at www.PromiselandOnline.com.

NOTES

Chapter 1. The Great Kid-Venture

1. Dr. Gilbert Bilezekian, quoted in the *Willow Creek Monthly* (October 1999), 3.

Chapter 2. Imagine the Best Hour

1. George Barna, *Barna Update—Teens and Adults Have Little Chance of Accepting Christ as Their Savior* (Ventura, Calif.: Barna Research Group, November 15, 1999).

Chapter 3. Your Mission, Should You Choose to Accept It . . .

1. *Apollo 13,* directed by Ron Howard (Universal Pictures, 1995).
2. Kay Kuzma, *Building Your Child's Character from the Inside Out* (Elgin, Ill.: David C. Cook, 1988), 2.
3. Karyn Henley, *Child Sensitive Teaching* (Cincinnati: Standard, 1997), 29.
4. Barna, *Barna Update.*
5. Prestonwood Baptist Church (Plano, Tex.), http://www.prestonwood.org (December 2002).
6. Grace Community Church (Carmel, Ind.), http://www.gracecc.org (December 2002).
7. Bill Hybels, Promiseland Conference general session—"The Difference One Children's Ministry Can Make" (South Barrington, Ill.: Willow Creek Association, 2002).
8. Mark Haguemen, (story told during the Promiseland Conference, South Barrington, Ill., Willow Creek Community Church, 2002).
9. John Ortberg, weekend message titled "Parents and Kids: Same Planet, Different Worlds—Hearts and Souls" (South Barrington, Ill.: Willow Creek Community Church, February 2003).

Chapter 4. The Big Six

1. Listen to "Don't Forget" from the CD *Dance, Shout & Sing* on the Web at www.PromiselandOnline.com.
2. Suzette Elgin, *The Gentle Art of Communicating with Kids* (New York: John Wiley & Sons, 1996), 9.

Chapter 5. Large Group, Small Groups, Big People

1. "God Is Eternal," a lesson in the Promiseland Curriculum, *5-G Challenge: Doing Life with God in the Picture. (South Barrington, Ill: Willow Creek Community Church, 2001).*
2. Marlene D. LeFever, *Learning Styles* (Colorado Springs: David C. Cook, 1995), 17.
3. Cynthia Ulrich Tobias, *The Way They Learn* (Colorado Springs: Focus on the Family, 1994), 99.
4. LeFever, *Learning Styles*, 18.

Chapter 6. Sharing the Dream

1. Bill Hybels, Leadership Summit general session—"The 'Y' Factor" (South Barrington, Ill.: Willow Creek Association, 2002).

Chapter 7. Lessons Learned

1. Stuart Hample and Eric Marshall, *Children's Letters to God* (New York: Workman, 1991).
2. Emily Kittle Morrison, *Leadership Skills* (New York: Fisher, 1994), 85.
3. Anne Allen Adams, Promiseland Conference general session—"Mobilize Volunteers for Maximum Impact (An Interview with the American Red Cross)" (South Barrington, Ill.: Willow Creek Association, 2003).

Chapter 8. Fit for the Adventure

1. Theodor S. Geisel (Dr. Seuss) and Audrey S. Geisel, *Oh, the Places You'll Go!* (New York: Random House, 1990).

2. John Maxwell, *The Maxwell Leadership Bible* (Nashville: Nelson, 2002), 300.

3. Aaron Niequist, "Bend My Knee." ©2000 Ever Devoted Music (admin. by Willow Creek Association). Used with permission. Listen to "Bend My Knee" on the Web at www.willowcharts.com.

4. C. S. Lewis, *The Letters of C. S. Lewis to Arthur Greeves*, quoted in Wayne Martindale and Jerry Root, *The Quotable Lewis* (Wheaton, Ill.: Tyndale House, 1989), 335.

5. Geisel and Geisel, *Oh, the Places You'll Go!*

Chapter 9. Sunday Morning Heroes

1. John F. Kennedy quoted in Ann Bausum, *Our Country's Presidents* (Washington, D.C.: National Geographic Society, 2001), 145.

2. Martin Luther King Jr., "Letter to Fellow Clergymen," quoted in Andrew Carroll, *Letters of a Nation* (New York: Kodansha America, 1997), 209.

3. Congressional Medal of Honor Society, http://www.cmohs.org (May 2003).

Appendix C

1. John Ortberg, Laurie Pederson, Judson Poling, *Pursuing Spiritual Transformation—Gifted to Serve* (South Barrington, Ill.: Willow Creek Associates, 1999), 33–34.

ACKNOWLEDGMENTS

Pat Cimo—Thanks for your love and leadership as my co-partner for the whole adventure.

Promiseland Staff—I can't imagine a better team to do life and ministry with than all of you.

Bill Hybels—Thanks for thirty years of leadership mentoring and deepening friendship. I love being a part of your team!

Fred Vojtsek—You and God get the credit for not letting me quit when things were really hard, so thanks.

David Staal—I am grateful for your passion, creativity, and tireless work on this book project. It would never gotten done without your gifts and talent.

My Family—For a lifetime of memories together, thanks. For the richness of life that I enjoy everyday, thanks. All of you are the loves of my life.

WILLOW
Willow Creek Association

Willow Creek Association
Vision, Training, Resources for Prevailing Churches

This resource was created to serve you and to help you build a local church that prevails. It is just one of many ministry tools that are part of the Willow Creek Resources® line, published by the Willow Creek Association together with Zondervan.

The Willow Creek Association (WCA) was created in 1992 to serve a rapidly growing number of churches from across the denominational spectrum that are committed to helping unchurched people become fully devoted followers of Christ. Membership in the WCA now numbers over 10,000 Member Churches worldwide from more than ninety denominations.

The Willow Creek Association links like-minded Christian leaders with each other and with strategic vision, training, and resources in order to help them build prevailing churches designed to reach their redemptive potential. Here are some of the ways the WCA does that.

- **Prevailing Church Conference**—an annual two-and-a-half day event, held at Willow Creek Community Church in South Barrington, Illinois, to help pioneering church leaders raise up a volunteer core while discovering new and innovative ways to build prevailing churches that reach unchurched people.

- **Leadership Summit**—a once-a-year, two-and-a-half-day conference to envision and equip Christians with leadership gifts and responsibilities. Presented live at Willow Creek as well as via satellite broadcast to over sixty locations across North America, this event is designed to increase the leadership effectiveness of pastors, ministry staff, volunteer church leaders, and Christians in the marketplace.

- **Ministry-Specific Conferences**—throughout each year the WCA hosts a variety of conferences and training events—both at Willow Creek's main campus and off-site, across the U.S. and around the world—targeting church leaders in ministry-specific areas such as: evangelism, the arts, children, students, small groups, preaching and teaching, spiritual formation, spiritual gifts, raising up resources, etc.

- **Willow Creek Resources**®—to provide churches with trusted and field-tested ministry resources in such areas as leadership, evangelism, spiritual formation, spiritual gifts, small groups, stewardship, student ministry, children's ministry, the use of the arts—drama, media, contemporary music—and more. For additional information about Willow Creek Resources® call the Customer Service Center at 800-570-9812. Outside the U.S. call 847-765-0070.

- *WillowNet*—the WCA's Internet resource service, which provides access to hundreds of transcripts of Willow Creek messages, drama scripts, songs, videos, and multimedia tools. The system allows users to sort through these elements and download them for a fee. Visit us online at www.willowcreek.com.

- *WCA News*—a quarterly publication to inform you of the latest trends, resources, and information on WCA events from around the world.

- *Defining Moments*—a monthly audio journal for church leaders featuring Bill Hybels and other Christian leaders discussing probing issues to help you discover biblical principles and transferable strategies to maximize your church's redemptive potential.

- *The Exchange*—our online classified ads service to assist churches in recruiting key staff for ministry positions.

- **Member Benefits**—includes substantial discounts to WCA training events, a 20 percent discount on all Willow Creek Resources®, access to a Members-Only section on WillowNet, monthly communications, and more. Member Churches also receive special discounts and premier services through WCA's growing number of ministry partners—Select Service Providers.

For specific information about WCA membership, upcoming conferences, and other ministry services contact:

Willow Creek Association
P.O. Box 3188, Barrington, IL 60011-3188
Phone: 847-570-9812
Fax: 847-765-5046
www.willowcreek.com

WELCOME TO PROMISELAND!

Transform your Sunday school into a powerful Children's Ministry! In Promiseland, kids establish a personal relationship with Christ and volunteers serve with great joy and passion. Promiseland is unique because it is entirely student-focused and fully utilizes small groups. Field-tested and refined at Willow Creek Community Church for over ten years, it is literally kid-tested and volunteer-approved!

Promiseland Builds Community

In Promiseland, children connect with loving adult volunteers who commit to care for them, disciple them, and help them become more like Christ.

Promiseland Is Fun

Kids love coming to Promiseland week after week, and often bring their friends! They form long-term relationships with adults and their peers in a joyful, energetic, and welcoming environment.

Promiseland Nurtures Faith

Through relevant Bible teaching, small group relation-ships, and the creative arts, Promiseland Curriculum lays a solid foundation of Bible knowledge and application. The two-year curriculum cycle provides six years of lessons in Christian discipleship for elementary students.

Promiseland Is Flexible

Promiseland offers thirteen sessions of Sunday or mid-week programming in Fall, Winter, and Spring quarterly kits for grades K/1, 2/3, and 4/5. During the Summer when attendance may be lower, or for smaller churches, Promiseland offers 10-session curriculum kits designed for a K-5 setting.

PROMISELAND CURRICULUM COMPONENTS

Promiseland Curriculum comes in quarterly kits (Fall, Winter, and Spring) that contain everything you need to minister to thirty kids for thirteen action-packed weeks! All student materials are reproducible, so as your attendance increases, you simply purchase additional guidebooks for your new adult leaders. Each curriculum kit contains:

- **Director's Notebook**—Promiseland overview pages; staffing information; small church adaptation ideas; Activity Station ideas; and the guidebooks for Administrators, Large Groups, and Small Groups.

- **Administrator's Guidebook**—Unit overview pages; a lesson-by-lesson checklist for administrative details; and all reproducible pages for handouts and take-home materials.

- **Large Group Programming Guidebook**— Unit overview pages; introduction to each Large Group program; and lesson-by-lesson instructions for Large Group Bible teaching.

- **Small Group Programming Guidebook**—Unit overview; introduction to Small Group discussions; and lesson-by-lesson instructions for Small Group activities and discussion.

- **Video**—includes selected drama lessons or video clips to enhance the Large Group teaching.

- **Special Features**—unique items that enhance the unit lessons, like a game, puzzle, or sound effects CD.

PROMISELAND CURRICULUM
QUARTERLY KITS

Promiseland Curriculum is divided into three grade levels (K/1, 2/3, 4/5) and two program years: God's Story: Genesis–Revelation and Doing Life With God in the Picture. Each program year has three quarters (Fall, Winter, Spring) and you can begin using it at any quarter.

God's Story: Genesis–Revelation gives kids a sequential view of the complete Bible so they can understand how people and events all fit together to tell God's Story. Retail Price: $299.00 per kit

Looking at the Pieces for Grades K/1

Fall Quarter	Winter Quarter	Spring Quarter
ISBN 0-744-11560-4	ISBN 0-744-11913-8	ISBN 0-744-11923-5

Making It Connect for Grades 2/3

Fall Quarter	Winter Quarter	Spring Quarter
ISBN 0-744-11567-1	ISBN 0-744-11932-4	ISBN 0-744-11941-3

It All Fits Together for Grades 4/5

Fall Quarter	Winter Quarter	Spring Quarter
ISBN 0-744-11575-2	ISBN 0-744-11950-2	ISBN 0-744-11958-8

Doing Life With God in the Picture teaches kids how to honor God in all areas of their lives through "The Five Gs" of Grace, Growth, Groups, Gifts, and Good Stewardship and begin their lifetime journey as fully devoted followers of Christ. Retail Price: $299.00 per kit

5-G Discovery for Grades K/1

Fall Quarter	Winter Quarter	Spring Quarter
ISBN 0-744-12365-8	ISBN 0-744-12368-2	ISBN 0-744-12371-2

5-G Challenge for Grades 2/3

Fall Quarter	Winter Quarter	Spring Quarter
ISBN 0-744-12366-6	ISBN 0-744-12369-0	ISBN 0-744-12372-0

5-G Impact for Grades 4/5

Fall Quarter	Winter Quarter	Spring Quarter
ISBN 0-744-12367-4	ISBN 0-744-12370-4	ISBN 0-744-12373-9

PROMISELAND CURRICULUM FOR INTEGRATED K-5 PROGRAMMING

These curriculum kits for grades K-5 are perfect for smaller churches, mid-week programs, church camps, summer Sunday School, or Vacation Bible School. Each kit contains ten sessions and includes Large Group teaching and Small Group discussion.

Camp Iwilligoway
I Will Live God's Way

Invite your kids to **Camp Iwilligoway** (i-WILL-uh-go-way) where they will learn about David, "a man after God's own heart," and discover how to trust, love, pray, obey, repent, believe, and worship God. This digital curriculum on CD-ROM includes reproducible student handouts, creative Bible teaching and Activity Station ideas, life application activities, and electronic clip art. There's also an audio CD with **Camp Iwilligoway** sound effects, narration, and 6 campfire songs.
ISBN 0-744-14459-0   Retail Price: $179.99

Metamorphosis
A God-Directed, Life Change Production

Kids will love the Insect-Inside Theatre Company's presentation of the book of Proverbs! **Metamorphosis** teaches children how to transform their attitudes, actions, words, and relationships according to biblical principles. The ten sessions on CD-ROM include video coaching, teaching options, Activity Station ideas, clip art, and "Before You Start" instructions. You also get an audio CD with the **Metamorphosis** Theme Song, Insect-Inside Theatre Welcome, sound effects, and story narrations for Large Group programs.
ISBN 0-744-13946-5   Retail Price: $179.99

Live the Adventure!
Discovering God is Everything I Need

Kids will explore the lives of heroes of faith like Joseph, Daniel, and Elijah to discover how God is their planner, protector, helper, provider, and forever friend. **Live the Adventure!** offers ten flexible-format sessions in print format with a Director's Guidebook, Administrator's Guidebook, Activity Stations Guidebook, Large Group Programming Guidebook, two Life Application Activities Guidebooks, drama video, and music CD.
ISBN 0-0310-23745-9   Retail Price: $249.99

We want to hear from you. Please send your comments about this book to us in care of zreview@zondervan.com. Thank you.

GRAND RAPIDS, MICHIGAN 49530 USA

WWW.ZONDERVAN.COM